# The

## Passionate

### Olive

2007

Dear Jindra,

Here's to life! love,
laughter — and,
olive oil! Jeanne —

All the best,
Carol Firenze

# The Passionate Olive

---

## 101 THINGS TO DO
## WITH OLIVE OIL

---

### Carol Firenze

BALLANTINE BOOKS | NEW YORK

A Note to Readers: *The Passionate Olive* contains a number of home remedies and solutions for common problems, including treatment of certain minor physical complaints. As with any such collection, the reader is urged to use common sense in following the suggestions in this book, particularly in the chapters entitled "To Your Health" and "Pregnancy and Baby Care with Olive Oil." In any situation where an underlying medical complaint may be the source of symptoms—**and in all situations where children and infants are concerned**—readers are strongly urged to consult with their physicians before undertaking any course of treatment or attempting any of the remedies described in *The Passionate Olive*. Wonderful and versatile as it is, olive oil should never be considered a substitute for appropriate medical treatment.

Published in the United States by Ballantine Books, an imprint of The Random House Publishing Group, a division of Random House, Inc., New York.

Ballantine and colophon are registered trademarks of Random House, Inc.

Owing to limitations of space, permission acknowledgments can be found on page 245, which constitutes an extension of this copyright page.

LIBRARY OF CONGRESS CATALOGING-IN-PUBLICATION DATA

Firenze, Carol.
The passionate olive / by Carol Firenze.—1st ed.
p. cm.
Includes bibliographical references and index.
ISBN 0-345-47676-X
1. Cookery (Olive oil)    2. Olive oil.
3. Olive oil—Health aspects.    I. Title.

TX819.O42F573 2005
641.3'463—dc22        2004052548

Printed in the United States of America

Ballantine Books website address: www.ballantinebooks.com

9  8  7  6  5

*To Jeff and Jaimie,*
*Victoria, Evan,*
*Isabella, and Christiana*
*with Love . . . and Olive Oil*

## ACKNOWLEDGMENTS

THERE ARE SO MANY PEOPLE who contributed their thoughts, experiences, and encouragement to this book that it is impossible to thank everyone in this short space. First of all, I would like to thank my dear friend and colleague Kathy Welch, who read every word of the manuscript, more than once, and masterfully added her ever-so-delightful comments. A special thank-you to Darrell Corti, who has spent a lifetime studying food, wine, and olive oil, for so graciously contributing his annotations to the book, and to olive oil expert Roberto Zecca, who offered guidance and whose name is mentioned to me in delightful conversations with olive oil producers wherever I go in my travels.

I would like to thank everyone's favorite cook, my mother Gigi Firenze, for her love of family and wonderful cooking, and for starting me on my path to being passionate about olive oil. She happily shared her family recipes and formulas. The other recipes are the brilliant work of Erik Cosselmon, executive chef of Kokkari Estiatorio in San Francisco, California—recently acclaimed as one of the *San Francisco Chronicle*'s "Best Restaurants in the Bay Area." A special thank-you to the first members of the

Extra Virgin Olive Oil Club: Midge Firenze, Ilse Palms, Marilee Irwin, Kathy Welch, and Marsha Felice; and ex-officio member Karry DeVincenzi Lensing, my cousin, who offered her cooking, health, and beauty tips. I would also like to thank Ellen Hongo and Watson, the basset hound, for pet recipes, and author Samantha Glen, who guided my journey toward publication.

A special thank-you to Maureen O'Neal and Johanna Bowman of Ballantine Books, and to my agent, Judith Riven, who believed in my book from the start and who is now religiously taking one tablespoon of extra virgin olive oil in the morning upon rising. Also to author Marlena de Blasi, who wrote the foreword, capturing her love of olive oil. Thanks to Paulo Lima, from the Italian Cooking & Living company; Jose Guerra and Elisabet Aguirre, from the Trade Commission for Spain; Patty Darragh and Bruce Golino from the California Olive Oil Council; Fabrizio Vignolini, director of the ONAOO; Xavier Marquès of NursTech, Inc.; Jennifer Lionti and Teresa D'Errico, from Colavita, USA; and Margie L. Preston of Interlace Design, for her magnificent and masterful watercolor illustrations.

Thank you to Dale Bryant, Mary Ursettie, Wareen Matukas, Maureen O'Connell, Emmy Moore Minister, Brenna Bolger, China Ziegenbein, Dylia Klatt, Hildy and Jim DeFrisco, Kareen Lambert, Marcia Riggio, Michael Bertoldo, Angela Di Blasi, Lillian Zappelli, Father Arthur Lenti, Rabbi Leslie Alexander, Kanella Sarros, Senia and Mark Feiner, Maria and Desmond Forbes, Brent Hewlett, Ralph Moceo (president of the Mostaccioli Club), Marge Bosetti, Keli Dietrich and Kristin Bosetti (who, at their own olive-oil weekend retreat, tested all of the beauty formulas), the John Bruzzone family (whose brainstormed list of olive oil uses are documented on a cocktail napkin), and Colleen Petersen, a non-Italian friend who, after reading the manuscript, asked "What's a *nonno*?" prompting me to explain Italian references.

Thank you to my *famiglia* and *amici* in Italy: Marta, Graziella, and Mauro Maurri, Anna Maria and Luciano Panero, Elisabetta Marchi, Patrizia and Massimo Cucchi, and Raffaella Sforza. And a special thanks to Walter McCall, DVM; Drs. Richard Coughlin, Irving Olender, and Catherine Grellet; Liz Summerhayes, NP, CNM, and . . . of course, to my favorite dermatologist.

And finally to my son, Jeff, his wife, Jaimie, and my four grandchildren—Victoria, Evan, Isabella, and Christiana—who, whenever a problem occurs, whether it be my son has an earache or my daughter-in-law has to polish an antique table for a special family dinner, or one of my granddaughters experiences a sunburn, or my grandson needs to take off his fake tattoos and fast! . . . *Nonna* Carol always has the cure. Just reach for the olive oil!

# CONTENTS

CHAPTER FIVE

*Beauty Is Skin Deep*    87

CHAPTER SIX

*Olive Oil and Sensuality*   111

CHAPTER SEVEN

*Pregnancy and Baby Care with Olive Oil*   125

CHAPTER EIGHT

## The Care and Feeding of Your Pets With Olive Oil    137

CHAPTER NINE

## Olive Oil Uses in Ritual, Religion, and Folk Magic    151

An Excerpt from *A Thousand Days in Tuscany* by
Marlena De Blasi

In her memoir *A Thousand Days in Venice*, Marlena De Blasi arrives in Italy as an American
tourist, marries the man of her dreams, and
makes Venice her new home. In the sequel, *A
Thousand Days in Tuscany*, she and her husband
pursue the country life in a small Tuscan village.
Here they attend the annual olive harvest, experience firsthand one of Italy's most beautiful and
sacred traditions, and passionately discuss the
elixir of the gods.

And now, plumped three meters up into the saddle of a
hundred-year-old tree, my bundled torso pitched about in
the gasping breath of early December, my wish is granted.
I'm harvesting olives.

Ears tingling under my old felt cloche, my fingertips
are white with cold as they slide in and out of Barlozzo's
gloves. . . . My nose runs. And all I do is send curses upon

Athena. It was she who, posturing with Poseidon for dominion, sprung the first olive tree from the stones of the Acropolis, proclaiming it the fruit of civility. A fruit like no other. She said the flesh of an olive was bitter as hate and scant as true love, that it asked work to soften it, to squeeze the golden-green blood from it. The olive was like life and that the fight for it made its oil sacred, that it would soothe and feed a man from birth until death. And the goddess's oil became elixir. Soft, slow drops of it nourished ewe's milk cheese; a ladle of it strengthened wild onions stewed over a twig fire. Burned in a clay lamp, oil illuminated the night, and warmed in the hands of a healer, it caressed the skin of a tired man and a birthing woman. Even now, when a baby is born in the Tuscan hills, he is washed in olive oil, modest doses burnished into every crease and crevice of him. On his deathbed, a man is anointed with the same oil, cleansing him in yet another way. And after he dies, a candle is lit and oil is warmed and kneaded over him, a farewell bath—the oil having accompanied him on all his journeys, just as Athena had promised. . . .

The olive mill is small, servicing only the local farmers or *padroni*, each of whom might have three or four hundred trees, less, perhaps, as Barlozzo's family does. The farmers often help each other to harvest, but there the sharing stops. Every farmer wants to be assured his olives—coddled and cared for better than anyone else's olives, harvested only at the moment of perfection—are pressed and returned to him as the jade fortune he deserves more than his neighbors do. . . . During what can be hours and hours of waiting for his own moments at the crusher, *il frantolano*, the olive mill owner, ministers to his clients. The mill is built for business: cement blocks and corrugated roofing, a dirt floor in part, smooth white tiles paving the machinery areas. Yet, in the end farthest from the fray, there is a great fireplace. . . . The farmers keep watch over their waiting olives, breaking the vigil with ritual refreshment. One whacks off a hunk of bread, roasts it on both sides over the embers, rubs it then with the garlic-rosemary branch, carries it, in his hand and with some ceremony, to the grunting press, and holds it under the spigot for a few seconds to let drip a thick sort of cream composed of the crushed but not yet pressed fruit. One carries his treasure back to the fire, to the demijohn, filling his tumbler with the thick, chewy wine of the countryside. . . .

And so we sit together, the farmers and their families and I, as if in the waiting room of a wizard. And all we talk of is olive oil. . . .

At one point, looking to build a bridge between the old world and the new, I open discourse about America, saying that the medical community advises the consumption of extra virgin olive oil to help lower the evil side of blood cholesterol. To a person, the circle looks at me with something near to mercy, and so I scurry on with the news of the American posture that touts the Mediterranean diet. "Constructed as it is of the freshest fruits and vegetables, complex carbohydrates, freshwater fish, sea fish, and a modicum of animal flesh—all of it laced with generous pourings of just-pressed olive oil and honest red wine—many American doctors call it the earth's healthiest eating plan."

Under darting gazes and fidgeting hands, I continue. "Of course, everyone knows that eating this way discourages heart disease and obesity, chases free radicals, and promotes longevity," I say, but there is no one even pretending to hear me. . . .

The mill owner has wandered over to the fire and caught the last of my feeble delivery. *"Ah, signora. Magari se tutto il mondo era d'accordo con noi.* How I wish that all the world agreed with us. Here people die of heart attacks, but most often in their beds and long past their nintieth birthdays."

Chuckles bustle through the crowd.

"But you have some experience with olive oil. I can see it," he says.

In reflex, my hand reaches up to touch my face. Are there telltale marks of last evening's supper?

"No, no, *signora*," says a man, perhaps the oldest one among the group. "There is no stain. He refers to your complexion. You have what we call here *pelle di luna*, skin like the moon. Your skin is illuminated. *È abbastanza comune qui*, it's fairly common here among the country women. It's the light that comes from eating olive oil all one's life. But is there olive oil in America?"

# Olive Oil Milestones

Around this time... this happened

6000 BC • Olive cultivation first appears in Syria

3000 BC • Knowledge and cultivation spreads in the Mediterranean area from east to west

2500 BC • Earthenware tablets in Crete reference olive oil and its uses

2000 BC • Ancient Israelites use precious olive oil for anointing priests and kings and to burn in temple lamps

1780 BC • The Code of Hammurabi states that, under penalty of death, no one can prune an olive tree more than two feet per year

1500 BC • Olive oil appears as a major commercial product in Crete and is sold in Egypt for use in cosmetics

1000 BC • The exceptional culinary aspects of olive oil are noted in Greece

776 BC • First Olympic Games take place where an olive branch and olive oil are awarded to the winners

620 BC • Solon's Olive Protection Law declares that anyone found guilty of uprooting or destroying an olive tree would be sentenced to death

100 BC • Greek and Roman literature reference olive trees, olives, and olive oil

| | |
|---|---|
| 100 AD | Romans develop several classifications of olive oil |
| 325 AD | Under the reign of Constantine, 2,300 oil distributors in the capital of the Empire supply citizens with olive oil for cooking, cosmetics, massage, body care, lamps, and other uses |
| 1000 AD | Olive oil becomes rare and is sometimes used as cash, but most of all is used for religious rituals |
| 1500– 1600 AD | Spanish explorers and missionaries carry the olive to the New World |
| 1524 AD | The first olive trees are planted in New Spain (Mexico) |
| LATE 1700– EARLY 1800 AD | Franciscan missionaries plant olive trees at nineteen of the twenty-one missions along 600 miles of the California coast |
| 1870 AD | Commercial olive oil production begins in California |
| 1900 AD | King Umberto I of Italy prohibits the felling of olive trees on Italian land—a law that still exists today in parts of Italy |
| 1920 AD | European immigrants to the United States begin to spread the use of olive oil into American cooking |
| 1980 TO PRESENT | Knowledge of olive oil expands worldwide as numerous books on health and cooking with olive oil are published |
| 2005 AD | *The Passionate Olive* touts the many uses of our magical, mystical, precious "liquid gold" |

# The

# Passionate

# Olive

# CHAPTER ONE

# *Liquid Gold*

OLIVE OIL . . . I JUST LOVE IT! I always have. I adore everything about it: the color, the feel, the taste, the texture, the variety, the mystique, the smell—the possibilities. I think my love of olive oil must be hereditary. Ever since I was a child growing up in an Italian American family, olives and olive oil have fascinated me. I remember opening a can of olives, draining the liquid, and putting whole pitted olives on my fingers and popping them in my mouth sequentially and eating them with complete delight. I also reminisce about my early childhood friends being shocked at our family's use of olive oil instead of the vegetable oils used in their homes, and their surprised faces as I dipped bread into oil rather than spreading it with butter. Even then I was trying to convert people to the magical world of olive oil.

All of my ancestors came from the region of Liguria, an area of Italy known for its light, flavorful, and delicate oils.

I remember savoring the exquisite tastes of my grand-mothers' cooking and hearing the stories about how my grandfathers saved money for several weeks to purchase the precious oil; it was a household priority and a staple and necessary for food as well as for many other practical things.

Throughout history there have been many people who have been completely amazed by the merits of olive oil. Although treating leprosy, massaging the skin of elephants, or boiling it to pour over castle walls onto attackers may not be counted among our current everyday uses for olive oil, its uses are not only infinite but also legendary. Homer was right when he named this precious oil *liquid gold* and sang praises to the olive tree in his epic poems.

While most people think of olive oil mainly as a culinary condiment, people of the ancient Mediterranean burned olive oil for illumination or applied it topically to the body. From ancient times to the present, people have used it for medicine, for magic, and as part of their everyday beauty rituals. Olive oil has always been more than a basic food to the people of the Mediterranean; it's been the Mediterranean's lifeblood and has illuminated history since the beginning of humanity.

Olive oil's mystical glow has been a magical ingredient in religious and spiritual rituals and a therapeutic resource to cure ailments and diseases. It was used to anoint kings (often poured directly on their heads), and it became a "monarch" itself when it became known as the king of all oils. In ancient Greece, athletes ritualistically smeared it all over their bodies before engaging in physical exercise, and winners were crowned with olive branch wreaths. In Rome, gladiators oiled their bodies as they prepared for competition. Celebrated physician and Father of Medicine Hippocrates recommended the use of olive oil for curing ulcers, cholera, and muscular pain. Drops were (and still are) trickled through holes in the tombs of saints to pay homage to them. Olive oil perhaps is the missing piece used in building one of the engineering wonders of the world, answering the question scholars have posed for centuries: *What else could have helped ease the movement of the great stones to build the pyramids of Egypt?*

The history of the olive culture mirrors the history of Western civilization. Although scholars disagree as to the actual specific location, the olive tree most likely originated in Asia Minor, probably in the Caucasus Mountains. What is known is that the first cultivated olive trees appeared around 6,000 BC in the area of Syria. They then spread to Crete, Palestine, and Israel. Much as precious petroleum oil is used as a basis for today's economy, back then the economy was based on the production and sale of grain, wine, and olive oil. As trading moved out into other regions, this commercial network spread the knowledge and cultivation to what is now Turkey, Cyprus, Egypt, and Greece.

By the seventh century BC, olive trees were well established in Greece. The olive tree was considered so sacred that legislation was written to prohibit the cutting down of one. Known as Solon's Olive Protection Law, and written by the statesman Solon, the law stated that anyone who uprooted or destroyed an olive tree would be judged in court and, if found guilty, sentenced to death. In fact, the olive culture was so highly valued and the fruit from trees considered so sacred and revered that only chaste men and virgins were authorized to pick the fruit. *(I wonder what kind of workforce we could gather today based on those stringent guidelines?)*

The Romans planted olive groves and extended olive cultivation throughout their ever-growing empire. They improved oil-production techniques by inventing what was to be the prototype of the modern lever press. Populations conquered by the Romans were often ordered to pay taxes in the form of olive oil. Why, you may ask? As great consumers of oil, the Romans could not feed their own citizens with local oil output (a situation that still exists in Italy today). As documented in the Museo dell'Olivo (the Carli Olive Tree Museum in Imperia, Italy), it has been estimated that adult citizens going to public gymnasiums used as much as 55 liters (14.3 gallons) of olive oil annually for personal hygiene, for consumption, as a lubricant, for lighting, for rituals, and as a medicament. That is a lot of olive oil!

The valuable oil played an important role in the development of the Mediterranean economy. Under Roman rule, the Mediterranean region was divided according to olive oil markets, and olive oil trading was as hot a commodity as was dot-com stock in its heyday. Two notable differences between the dot-com peak and the olive oil peak: First of all, according to the historian Pliny, by the first century AD, Rome had excellent oil that was sold "at reasonable prices." Second, olive oil is a trend that has lasted.

Advanced ships were built for the purpose of transporting oils a great distance. Hispania (that portion of the Roman Empire encompassing most of present-day Spain and Portugal) was the largest supplier of this precious liquid, and its olive oils were considered the holy grail of oils and thought to have the finest quality. The oil was shipped in terra-cotta amphoras (large, two-handled jars with narrow necks). Often carrying up to seventy kilos of olive oil, these amphoras could be used only once for three major reasons: olive oil permeated the porous terra-cotta causing rancidity if used again; they often became damaged during the voyage; and cleaning and recycling the amphoras was unprofitable. The number of discarded amphoras is staggering. In fact, there is a mountain in Rome called Mt. Testaccio—forty-nine meters high and one kilometer wide—that is made entirely of methodically broken, discarded, and stacked amphoras.

The citizens of Rome and other parts of this vast empire consumed great quantities of Hispania's wonderful oil. Even the oldest cookbook (that we know about), written by Apicius in the first century AD and entitled *De Re Coquinaria* ("On Cookery"), included many recipes using Hispania's oil.

Olive cultivation declined during the barbarian invasions. It became rare and valuable during the Middle Ages, where it was chiefly used for religious purposes. Religious orders owned a great share of the cultivated olive trees, and behind monastic walls the precious oil could be found at the tables of churchmen.

The history of olive cultivation in the New World can be traced to missionaries traveling with Spanish explorers and conquistadors who carried the olive to Mexico (New Spain), to Caribbean settlements, then to the mainland of South America (Peru, Paraguay, Argentina, Chile), and, at last, to what is now California. As early as 1524, Franciscan missionaries planted olive trees in New Spain. As they prepared for new settlements (in Baja California), they would take pot cuttings (or seeds) from existing orchards to their new outposts.

Sailing in the name of Spain, Italian explorer Christopher Columbus, while not involved in olive agriculture, noted the importance of olive oil during his journey to the New World. He is said to have allotted a daily ration of a quarter liter of olive oil (about 1 cup) to each sailor aboard ship.

The early history of olive cultivation in present-day California revolves around the Franciscan fathers. During the second half of the eighteenth century and early nineteenth century, olive groves were established at nineteen of the twenty-one California missions, beginning with San Diego de Alcala and ending with San Francisco Solano Mission in Sonoma. Only the missions at San Francisco and Carmel do not have suitable climates for growing olive trees.

Historically, the original purpose of growing olives in California was for the making of oil, with the first oil produced in 1803. By the mid-nineteenth century, olive oil was a thriving industry, but then it languished. Its popularity was cyclical, and, by the end of the nineteenth century, table olives became the primary products from the fruit of the tree (and still are). However, in recent years, a number of Californians are planting olive trees and harvesting the fruit to make exceptional olive oil.

Since 1985, the use of olive oil in the United States has grown exponentially with the importing of excellent European oils, the availability of award-winning California oils, the national focus on health and nutrition, and the growing interest in culinary arts. But not too many people know that the olive tree itself has always been a symbol of abundance, peace, longevity, and wisdom.

Capable of living up to three thousand years, this hardy and undemanding tree can survive semi-arid climates, shallow soil, and decapitation. Should a tree die, shoots will begin to grow from the base. Because of its immortal nature, the tree and the oil produced from it have developed magical auras and are referenced in numerous legends, stories, and myths.

## Mythical, Mystical, and Legendary

The olive tree has inspired myths and legends and has enjoyed an unrivaled degree of fame (well, with perhaps the possible exception of the grapevine). It was especially lauded during the Greek, Egyptian, and Roman eras. In Greece, the history of olive oil is as old as the gods of Olympus. One Greek legend accounts for the very origin of the olive and associates it with the founding of the city of Athens. According to the legend, a contest was held in Greece to see which god or goddess would be the patron of the new Greek city. Athena, goddess of wisdom, was challenged by Poseidon, god of the sea and horses, to provide the Greeks with the most useful, divine gift. Poseidon produced the horse; however, Athena was chosen by Zeus as the winner of the contest because she provided the most useful gift—the olive tree—noted for its oil, fruit, and wood and as the symbol of peace, wisdom, and prosperity. Even today, an olive tree stands where the story of this legendary competition is said to have taken place. The myth lives on; it is said that all the olive trees in Athens were descended from that first olive tree offered by Athena.

Throughout Greece, competitions were held in close connection with the olive tree. The Olympic Games, held in honor of Zeus, are where Olympic athletes (massaged with olive oil) believed that wisdom, power, and strength would be bestowed upon them. It was also believed that if one polished a statue of Zeus with olive oil, he would be so honored that he would bring the statue owner a long and happy life.

In Egypt, the kingdom that worshiped its pharaohs in life as well as death, crowns of olive branches were ritually offered and placed in tombs. Olive oil, mixed with sesame and pistachio oils, was applied prior to the linen wrapping of a mummy. The ancient Egyptians, who also used olive oil for cosmetics and medicine, believed the olive tree to be a gift from the gods that would bestow beauty, power, and love to its users. They also believed that Isis, goddess of fertility and wife of Osiris, a supreme god of the Egyptians, was responsible for teaching man how to extract oil from olives.

However, always competitive, the Romans credit the olive tree and its oil to their goddess of wisdom, technical skill, and invention—Minerva—who, according to legend, gave the Romans the art of cultivating the olive tree. The legendary founders of Rome—the twins Romulus and Remus—were believed to have been born under an olive tree. Another legend attributes the wild olive tree to Hercules, who struck the ground with his mighty club, which then took root. Whatever the legends, the *civilized* Romans, to this day, are credited with saying: *"Partes humani cultus necessariae vinum . . . atque oleum olivarum"*—"The necessary ingredients of civilization are wine and . . . olive oil."

# Moses, Christ, and Muhammad Have One Thing in Common

Olive oil occupies a central place in all of the religions associated with the Mediterranean and the Middle East. The oil has been used for lamps in temples and for anointing rituals since time immemorial. Olive oil was sacred to Moses, Christ, and Muhammad.

Olive oil is referenced more than 140 times in the Bible, and the olive tree, considered the king of all trees, is mentioned over one hundred times. In Genesis, an olive branch was returned to Noah on the ark by a dove, signaling the end of the great flood. Since then, the olive branch has been viewed as a symbol of life and peace. The greatest religious significance of olive oil is documented in the book of Exodus, where the Lord tells Moses how to make an anointing oil of spices and olive oil. The olive tree and olive oil permeate different ancient psalms and prayers, many of which are recited today, including Psalm 23:5, ". . . you anoint my head with oil."

For the Jewish people, having a plentiful supply of oil, along with wine, was a symbol of God's favor. Oil was, and still is, a sign of God's blessing because it represents all that is best in life and God's generosity to the people he loves.

In the Christian churches, both Western (Roman Catholic and Protestant) and Eastern (Orthodox), olive oil is the symbol of God's boundless generosity toward humankind and of his never-ending love. Christ (Christós) means the anointed one, that is, anointed with (olive) oil. When it is used to anoint people in church, it becomes one of the channels through which God's power comes into the world and by which he blesses Christians with his Holy Spirit.

The olive and its oil hold a special position in the Greek Orthodox religion. As a symbol of love and peace, olive oil is an essential part of several solemn rites, including baptism. It is also used to light the oil lamps in churches and the small shrines in many Greek households. In fact, the Greek word for olive, *elaía*, is thought to be derived from the noun *eleos*, which has many meanings, including mercy and compassion. In the Eastern Church, as well as in the Western Church, a prayer that is continuously offered is "*Kyrie eleison,*" Greek for "Lord have mercy." The verb *eleison* is related to *eleos* (mercy and compassion) and to *elaion* (olive oil). This relationship suggests that—at a deeper level of meaning—olive oil is a material manifestation of Christ's blessing.

In Islam, the olive tree is a symbol of Muhammad's presence, and, through the oil, divine light brings men closer to Allah. In the Koran (Qur'an) and in the Hadiths (sayings of the Prophet) there are many references to olive oil. Muhammad is said to have advised his followers to apply olive oil to their bodies and to "use olive oil as a food and ointment for it comes from a blessed tree" (Tirmidi). In one Hadith, the Prophet was said to have stated that olive oil has in it a cure for seventy diseases: "Eat the olive oil and apply it (locally), since there is cure for seventy diseases in it, one of them is Leprosy" (Abu Naim).

## Virgin or Refined . . . It's All About Culture

The olive tree is an icon of beauty and resistance; in olive cultures one of the cruelest things you can say about someone is that he is the kind of person who would cut down an olive tree.

Looking at an olive tree with its silvery-green leaves, twisted trunk, and graceful branches, gives one a feeling of peace and serenity. The gnarled and knotty trunk looks as old as humanity, yet the leaves represent youthful gentleness as they gracefully sway. The olive tree is perhaps the most favored of trees by artists. Fascinated by their beauty, Matisse, Renoir, Cézanne, and Dali have all painted olive trees. The master of them all was van Gogh, whose olive tree paintings number nineteen.

## Get Healthy, Stay Young, and Enjoy

Olive oil was first used *on* the body, not *in* it. For centuries, olive oil has been used to maintain the suppleness of skin, to heal abrasions, to soften the hair, to strengthen nails, to cure the effects of alcohol, and to relieve aching muscles. It wasn't until about 1,000 BC that the exceptional culinary benefits of olive oil were discovered.

Recent research has brought olive oil back into the health annals, making it a primary focus among health-conscious people as they rediscover its culinary, beauty, and health benefits. In addition to lending a distinctive taste to Mediterranean cuisine, this versatile fruit and its oil have been found to reduce cholesterol—a truly healthful benefit! Olive oil can also help prevent cardiac diseases, ease the pain of arthritis, and soothe intestinal disorders.

In addition, ingesting (in food) or drinking (by the spoonful or glass) olive oil, with its potent supply of vitamins A, D, K, and E, is thought to slow down the aging process. Olive oil contains antioxidants, which are powerful aids that can help keep the cardiovascular system flowing and delay the aging of cells. Olive oil aids digestion and helps the body absorb calcium. It improves the appearance and texture of the skin . . . all from the inside.

Now for the outside of the body: Just as the gladiators believed that using olive oil for massage maintained the elasticity of muscles and the soldiers of Greece oiled their skin to keep warm, applying olive oil to the skin has been shown to improve its appearance and texture.

So enjoy your olive oil, however you use it. Having the knowledge of its history and culture, its spiritual significance and infinite virtues, and its health and beauty benefits, you can now play with this "liquid gold" and know that in addition to its epicurean enjoyment it offers 101 ways to improve your life, love, and health.

# CHAPTER TWO

# *Virgin or Refined?*

A NUMBER OF YEARS AGO, when Kuleto's Restaurant in San Francisco began putting tiny bottles of olive oil on their tables and the local culinary community took to dipping their bread rather than spreading, I formed a special club called EVOOC (Extra Virgin Olive Oil Club). Its membership consisted of my closest friends. Our very informal club centered on convivial conversation, great bread, and olive oil—naturally! When I worked and lived in London and traveled extensively throughout Europe, I introduced many of my colleagues to EVOOC and they became lovers of olive oil. EVOOC has changed little over the years—just several new members and a new name, the Passionate Olives Club.

Today, it seems as if olive oil is everywhere—from your local corner grocery to the gourmet kitchen shop to those huge discount and wholesale stores. There are literally shelves and shelves of olive oils. We find olive oil on tables at restaurants, in soaps and creams at the beauty counter, and on monthly (or in my case, weekly) shopping lists. For those of you who might think that olive oil is just another type of oil, you have *much* to learn.

When you go to the store, do you wonder which kind to buy? What type do you use and when? How can you be certain in your selection of a given oil, and should you care if it is extra virgin or if it is simply olive oil that has been refined? You may have already asked yourself these questions, as Bruce Tindall and Mark Watson did in their book *How Does Olive Oil Lose Its Virginity?*

## *Let's Begin . . .*

Stepping back into history, one finds that olive oil has been classified according to its quality for centuries. The Romans used to classify olive oil into five categories, with the socially designated upper classes (priests, nobles, and athletes) privileged to enjoy the very best of the oil and the slaves destined to have the oil extracted from rotten olives. *Talk about an unfair class system!* The Romans' five designated categories were:

- *Oleum ex albis ulivis:* oil extracted from green olives
- *Oleum viridum:* oil extracted from olives beginning to color or ripen
- *Oleum maturum:* oil extracted from ripe or mature olives
- *Oleum caducum:* oil extracted from olives that have fallen to the ground
- *Oleum cibarium:* oil extracted from rotten olives or olives

with worms (it is interesting to note that the word *cibar-ium* also refers to "food")

Since that time the classifications and definitions have gone through many iterations, including the designations of virgin oil as "sweet oil," or "sweet oyl" in some early references, for late-harvested olives. Even today, olive oils may be distinguished by their quality and by the subtle and not-so-subtle differences in varieties, flavors, and aromas. Still, the primary distinction of extra virgin olive oil is its lack of defects.

Most olive oil–producing countries use a set of designated standards to grade their olive oil. The European Union, as the leading world producer, generating over 80 percent (and consuming 70 percent) of the world's olive oil, has led the way for new regulations that focus on clear definitions and labels. New international standards (beginning with the fall harvest of 2003) have been adopted by the International Olive Oil Council (IOOC), an intergovernmental organization headquartered in Madrid, Spain, that focuses on maintaining the integrity of the olive industry worldwide.

## Definitions

To the neophyte olive oil consumer (and even to those who have grown up with olive oil by their side), the classifications of olive oil can be confusing. Depending upon the rules and legal regulations of the different countries throughout the world, not all classifications are sold directly to the consumer. In addition, some countries require more specific designations and labeling. I am presenting brief descriptions of only three olive oils (two virgins and one refined) and one olive-pomace oil that you will most likely find in a store or on the Internet.

Please note that I am *not* defining all the grades of olive oil or olive-pomace oil *nor* presenting a highly detailed chemical composition or gas chromatography for each classification of olive oil. Those readers who want additional information should log on to the IOOC website (www.internationaloliveoil.org) or the California Olive Oil Council's website (www.cooc.com).

## Olive Oil

The classification of *Olive Oil* means that it is an oil that is obtained only from the fruit of the olive tree. It is not mixed with any other oils (for example, hazelnut oil), and the process by which it is made cannot involve the use of solvents or reesterification (one definitely needs a college chemistry course to understand this!). The classification of *Olive Oil* is further divided into *Virgin Olive Oil* and *Olive Oil.*

In order for an olive oil to bear the classification of *virgin*, the oil must be obtained only by mechanical means or other physical means, under specific temperature or thermal requirements that do not lead to its alteration or deterioration. Any treatment other than washing, decantation, centrifugation, or filtration is not acceptable. There are several grades of virgin olive oil. Here are the two that you are probably familiar with:

- *Extra Virgin Olive Oil* means that the oil has been made by mechanical means, its free acidity (oleic acid) is not more than 0.8 percent, and the oil has no defects. Many countries are now requiring specific labeling regulations—for example, the label requirement for extra virgin olive oil reads: "This is an olive oil of superior category produced directly from olives and only through mechanical processes."

- *Virgin Olive Oil* means that its free acidity (oleic acid) is not more than 2 percent, and there may be minor defects. Virgin olive oil is also made by mechanical means.

Let's leave the virgin classification and the two grades described above and move on to the other classification under *Olive Oil: Olive Oil.* Yes, to add to the confusion, the overall classification of *Olive Oil* (meaning oil made solely from the fruit of the olive tree) is different from the designation or grade called *Olive Oil.*

- *Olive Oil,* as a grade, means that it is a blend of refined and virgin olive oil. It has a free acidity (oleic acid) of not more than 1 percent. Regulations in some countries require labeling on olive oil to read: "Oil containing exclusively olive oil which has undergone a refining process and oil produced directly from olives."

Refined means that defects, found in the base oil, are removed and that the oil is blended with extra virgin or virgin olive oil. Solvents are not used to extract the oil, but it has been refined with the use of charcoal and other chemical and physical filters.

# Olive-Pomace Oil

*Olive-Pomace Oil* is obtained by treating olive pomace (the pulpy material that remains after the pressing of olives) with solvents or other physical treatments. The grade of *Olive-Pomace Oil* sold to consumers consists of a blend of refined olive-pomace oil and virgin olive oil. You will notice that the term *olive oil* is not used in this classification because it cannot be applied to olive-residue oils. Some countries forbid the sale of olive-pomace oil for consumption. Although olive-pomace oil is sometimes used for cooking (I don't think it should be!), those who are interested in quality cooking and baking would never use this oil.

# First Cold Pressed and Cold Extraction

Other terms we often see on labels are *first cold pressed* and *cold extraction.* If a label reads "first cold pressed," the oil must have been produced from the first pressing of olives with a traditional hydraulic press at a temperature of less than 27°C (80.6°F).

The term *cold extraction* refers to oil produced at temperatures of less than 27°C (80.6°F) using an extraction system that is not a hydraulic press. It can be a percolation system (Sinolea) or a centrifugal system (decanting centrifuge).

While various producers passionately disagree about

which technology is the best, it appears that the less heat and the quicker and more careful the extraction, the better the oil. However, there may be oils labeled "cold pressed" that are made not using a hydraulic press. The designation description "cold pressed" does not guarantee a superior olive oil.

## Filtered and Unfiltered

Other terms we hear are "unfiltered" and "filtered." "Unfiltered" oil looks opaque or hazy because tiny particles of the fruit are still suspended in the oil and will sink to the bottom of the bottle over time. These particles are removed in "filtered" oil by a process using cotton wool or filter paper that traps the small particles of the fruit and fruit water. Serious tasters and producers prefer "unfiltered" oil because they feel it is better protected against oxidation and tastes more lively and vibrant. However, a good quality extra virgin olive oil tastes delicious whether filtered or unfiltered.

## Estate Grown, Blended, and Light Olive Oils

Other labels we often come across include "estate grown," "blended," "light olive oil," or even "extra light olive oil." In California, "estate grown" means that at least 95 percent of the oil must be derived from a particular estate. "Blended olive oil" is produced by combining olive oils from different geographical origins or different cultivars.

We also see the terms *light olive oil* and *extra light olive oil.* These terms are often used as marketing ploys. Consumers may think that "extra" means "extra virgin," which it does not, and may think that "light" refers to fewer calories, which it does not. "Light" does *not* mean fewer calories; all oil has the same number of calories: 120 per tablespoon. These are refined oils that are lighter in color, fragrance, and taste.

## The Problem with the Classifications . . . But There Is Good News

The trouble with these various definitions is that not all countries (including the United States) use European Union regulations or IOOC standards. Theoretically, a producer can chemically refine an olive oil and label it "extra virgin," or an importer can label inferior oil as "extra virgin." The good news is that there is a law that requires a label to include the country of origin of the oils. It is not enough to merely indicate "imported from" or "packed in," the label must specify where the oils originated. Read labels! You may think you are buying an Italian olive oil, only to discover on the back of the label a line reading: "Packed in Italy with oils of Italy, Spain, Greece, and Tunisia."

Another note of good news is that several regions,

states, and countries issue seals and certifications of authenticity of origin and specific standards for their extra virgin olive oils. In the United States, California issues the COOC (California Olive Oil Council) seal; for Italian oils, look for DOP (Denominazone di Origine Protetta), translated as PDO (Protected Designation of Origin), and IPG (Indicazione Geografica Protetta), translated as PGI (Protected Geographical Indication); for Greek oils, look for PDO (Protected Designation of Origin); for French oils, the designation is AOC (Appellation d'Origine Contrôlée); and for Spanish oils, the DO (Denominación de Origen) initials will appear.

COOC SEAL OF AUTHENTICITY

In the United States, the COOC works with its own certified tasting panel and issues the COOC seal to those oils that achieve the IOOC extra virgin olive oil rating. The IOOC has accredited experts and "taste panels" that operate in various participating producer countries; it has given them the specific task of certifying that oils are truly extra virgin olive oils according to IOOC organoleptic (taste and aroma) specifications. The first California official olive oil panel of tasters was certified in 2001 by the

IOOC. The COOC, in cooperation with the University of California at Davis extension, created this panel. Headed by Roberto Zecca and Paul Vossen, it meets several times a month to judge whether submitted California olive oils meet the IOOC standards and can accurately be labeled "extra virgin olive oil"—that is, oil without any defects.

A tasting panel conducts blind organoleptic evaluations of olive oils and makes a determination based upon the presence or absence of defects. Specific adjectives are used to describe both the positive attributes and the major defects of the oils sampled. The positive attribute taste descriptors are fruity (*fruttato*), bitter (*amaro*), and pungent (*piccante*). Descriptors, used to describe the sensory perception of defects, include fusty, musty, winey-vinegary, muddy sediment, metallic, and rancid. The IOOC provides certified tasting panels with detailed instructions and a standard assessment form, called a Profile Sheet, which is used to document the judging of extra virgin olive oil.

Annual olive oil competitions abound in many olive oil–producing countries. Major competitions in Europe include the Leone D'Oro and L'Orciolo D'Oro, both of which are international, and the Ercole Olivario, which is open only to estate-produced Italian oils. The only competition held in the United States is the Olive Oils of the World competition at the Los Angeles County Fair each May, where a team, including world-renowned official tasters, meets to taste and judge. At this competition, the Sensory Assessment profile analysis is used to award gold, silver, and bronze medals for extra virgin olive oil. The late Dr. Mario Solinas, a former professor at the University of Perugia, developed the assessment analysis several years ago. He was the first researcher to provide a common approach in defining and analyzing the positive aspects and qualities of extra virgin olive oil.

## Still a Bit Confused?

Stick to extra virgin olive oil for fine cooking. A true connoisseur of olive oil knows that extra virgin is the best in terms of quality and taste. It should exhibit an "olive fruity" taste, ranging from light to medium to intense. Just as wines vary according to varietals of grapes, climatic conditions, and soil attributes, olives, too, have many varying qualities that affect the oil they ultimately produce. There are, as well, the variations in color and in taste, due to the time of harvest, different methods of oil extraction, the regions and climatic conditions, and different olive cultivars.

There are approximately 2,500 types of olives worldwide, 431 in Italy alone. In each growing region (note, I did not say country) there are distinctive cultivars. For example, the most well-known olives for olive oil production in central Italy around Tuscany, Umbria, and the Marche are Frantoio, Leccino, Pendolino, and Moraiolo olives. In Liguria, it is the Taggiasca; in southern Italy, around Puglia, Abruzzo, and Molise, are the Coratina and Ogliarola olives; and in Sicily, the Giraffa and Nocellera olives. In Greece, in the Peloponnesus, the Kalamata (Kalamon) olive reigns supreme; and on Crete, it is the Koroneiki. In Catalonia, Spain, the Arbequina is the popular olive grown for oil production; in southern Spain, the Hojiblanca is common; but the Picual accounts for over 50 percent of the olives grown in Spain (the world's largest olive oil–producing country). When any of these olive trees are grown in different geographic regions (for example, in California), they may produce slightly different flavors.

## So How Do You Decide?

With all of the olive oil products on the market, it is good to become familiar with the various labeling descriptors. Remember to look for the "use by" date. Once opened, olive oil should optimally be used within sixty to ninety days. Always check for the country of origin (of the olives and the oil) and look for specific seals or marks of authenticity. This can help you in your buying decisions. Also, more important, a reputable retailer can answer your questions and guide you.

Yet in the end, even after all the tasting, testing, reading, studying, and discussing . . . what tastes, smells, looks, and feels best to you is the olive oil you should use and enjoy.

## You May Ask, But What Types of Olive Oil Do I Use and When?

As you read other chapters of *The Passionate Olive: 101 Things to Do with Olive Oil*, you will notice frequent references to the classification or type of olive oil to use in a given recipe or formula. I find the best rule of thumb is to use extra virgin olive oil for cooking, for that morning tablespoon (more about *that* later), and for most applications directly on the skin—whether adult, baby, or pet. Extra virgin olive oil is superior in terms of quality and taste and antioxidant benefits. For other health and beauty uses, including those on the hair, in the bath, or in the ears, a virgin olive oil or olive oil can be used. Of course, extra virgin olive oil works for these uses as well; that's what I usually use. For tasks in and around the house, use a refined and less-expensive olive oil. I have also included a chart of Suggested Types of Olive Oil for 100 Uses and a chart of Suggested Types of Olive Oil for Cooking in the Olive Oil Usage Guidelines section of the book.

In subsequent chapters, food recipes and formulas are shaded. An icon with a bottle of olive oil surrounded by vegetables designates a recipe for you, your friends, or your pet—something to be consumed. The icon with two bottles of olive oil surrounded only by olive leaves designates formulas for external uses only.

Now that you have learned about the many types of olive oil available, the stage is set for you to learn of the many uses for this golden liquid—many of which have been handed down in my family for literally generations. So, grab your favorite bottle (of olive oil) and let's begin our adventure around the house, exploring the amazing diversity of this practical substance.

# CHAPTER THREE

# Around the House

EVEN AS A LITTLE GIRL, I was aware of the many magical uses of olive oil. I often noticed my parents, grandparents, aunts, and uncles taking the gallon-sized can of olive oil out of the kitchen to use in various daily household tasks—whether the tasks involved cleaning, preservation, prevention, maintenance, repair, or just something that needed attention "in a pinch." I marveled at the stories they told of the importance of olive oil—like the story of the famous Italian American baseball player Joe DiMaggio. It seems as if olive oil might have actually contributed to his fame. When he started playing baseball in 1931, an olive oil distributor named Rossi sponsored his first team. And as I understand it, Joe DiMaggio rubbed olive oil on his bat (his baseball bat, of course!) and often soaked it in olive oil for up to ten days. The treatment purportedly gave his bat greater spring!

To this day, whenever I mention my love of olive oil,

some people stare at me in amazement, while others gleefully tell me how they use it. At a recent dinner party, I sat next to a young woman who manages a furniture store. She told me that prior to the store's professional photo shoots, the furniture is polished with olive oil. The extra sheen provided by the olive oil makes the furniture pop off the pages of their high-end catalog. The mahogany simply gleams! I listen to these stories and fondly remember my childhood and the glistening mahogany furniture in my grandparents' homes.

I grew up in a large, colonial-style home in what was then considered the country; it is now part of one of the trendiest areas in Silicon Valley. Yet at the time, the house was quite remote from the city, with little traffic to disturb the stillness of the night. It had wonderful large rooms in which every sound would reverberate. Its heavy doors were characteristic of the fine 1928 construction. In older homes, creaks and noises can be a bit frightening to a young girl in the middle of the night. I remember my father using drops of olive oil (no WD-40 in those days!) to prevent the creaks and squeaks, thus assuring the family a restful night's sleep. It worked! In fact, any gears or hinges around the house can be oiled with this magical substance. After all, if the Romans applied olive oil to the wooden and metal mechanisms of their weaponry, and if workers during the Industrial Revolution lubricated some machines with olive oil, why not oil the gears and hinges around your home with same golden liquid?

As an adult, I remember the day I had a "fashion crisis" and couldn't seem to find anything in the house to solve the problem. I was on my way out the door to attend a family member's wedding when I made one last quick stop to check my lipstick in the hall mirror. I saw that the pearls I had chosen for the event had lost a great deal of their beautiful luster. Realizing that I had absolutely no cleaners around the house that did not contain some type of harsh chemical, I wondered what I could possibly do to revitalize my pearls. I was uncomfortable using anything harsh for fear of damaging them. It suddenly came to me to get out my trusty bottle of olive oil. I poured a small amount on a kitchen towel and rubbed it onto my pearls. To my delight and pleasure, they soon glowed the way they did when I first received them from a dear relative. I was so happy that I had thought to use my old standby, olive oil . . . it's *always* there in a pinch.

Besides all the practical uses for olive oil, another major reason to reach for the golden liquid in lieu of the many commercial cleaning products currently on the market is our health. Consider for a moment the warning labels placed on chemical-based cleaning products—even the organic alternatives. Many of them clearly state that they can be quite dangerous if used "incorrectly." Protecting yourself, your family, and the environment from toxic chemicals is much easier than you think. There is a safe, natural alternative to the many hostile chemical- and petroleum-based cleaning products and polishes. That's right—just reach for the olive oil!

How many times have you walked down the cleaning products aisle in a grocery store and marveled at the sheer number of different bottles, cans, and aerosol sprays available for cleaning and polishing? Whenever I see people buying so many different products, I imagine their returning home and cramming the various liquids and sprays in their limited cabinet space. I want to tap them on the shoulder and mention that one of the only products they need around the house (that is environmentally safe, effective, *and* simple to use) is olive oil. You can simplify your life, your shopping, and your housekeeping by adopting olive oil as a partner in your everyday routines. While olive oil cannot be used for every cleaning chore, it can be used on many of them as it does the job of cleaning, polishing, lubricating, waterproofing—and so much more. Another great reason for using olive oil? It can cost less than other store-bought chemical cleaning products. And it really works!

What follows are some practical and economical uses for the golden oil that olive cultures have used for centuries to handle some of the most common problems around the house. And now . . . on to the list:

## Cleaning with Olive Oil

### 1) CLEAN AND POLISH SLATE, TILE, AND HARDWOOD FLOORS

It seems as if I am always cleaning something around the house with the help of olive oil. And if your home is like mine, there is no end to the things that need constant cleaning attention. For example, let's start with what is right under our feet every day—the floors. Whether they are tile, slate, or hardwood floors, they need to be cleaned on a regular basis to keep them shining. My cousin, Graziella, who lives near Genoa, Italy, has beautiful charcoal-colored slate floors throughout her very modern home. She told me that she keeps them shining and clean with the regular use of olive oil. I have dark hardwood floors in my hallway and tile floors in my kitchen. After sweeping the floors to remove all of the large particles of dirt and dust, I apply several drops of olive oil and several drops of lemon juice on a dry mop or cloth broom and oil mop the floors. Any remaining small particles of dust will cling to the mop or broom. If you have just washed the floors, you can always use the oil as a follow-up treatment. Your floor will be positively gleaming and will be much cleaner with this process. Remember, only a few drops each of olive oil and lemon juice will do the trick!

## 2) CLEAN PEWTER

Entertaining family and friends is a well-known tradition among Italians, Greeks, and other Mediterranean/olive cultures. Any excuse for a get-together is seized upon with great enthusiasm. Along with the all-important food preparation is the preparation of one's home to receive guests. Both of these preparty preparation steps include the use of a great deal of olive oil. Whenever I give a party, I get out my *nonna* Jenny's beautiful pewter serving plates and candleholders. To make sure they are seen at their very best, I use her ancient recipe for cleaning them. Olive oil can clean anything in the house that is made of pewter, including chargers (those decorative plates, used under china dinner plates, which can often become stained). *Nonna*'s recipe for cleaning pewter will work for other types of metals, too, but more about that later.

*Nonna's Pewter Cleaning Formula*

- Mix ½ cup of olive oil and 2 tablespoons of baking soda
- Dip a dry cloth into the olive oil mixture
- Rub the cloth onto the pewter and the spots will disappear. See your precious pewter shine!

### 3) CLEAN WAX OFF CANDLEHOLDERS

Once the family pewter candleholders are clean and shining, my *nonna* also taught me a secret about how to prevent wax from forming on the interior of a candleholder with . . . what else . . . olive oil. Placing a few drops of olive oil into the interior of the candleholder will prevent the buildup of wax. We have all had the experience of removing candle wax from a candleholder the day after a party, and this trick makes this often time-consuming task a breeze! But let's get back to the party—I'll even share one of the recipes.

*Nonna's Famous Recipe for Chicken Fricassée*

6 chicken thighs

3 tablespoons extra virgin olive oil

1 yellow or white onion

1 clove garlic

1 tablespoon parsley

Pinch of dried (or fresh) herbs (oregano, thyme, marjoram)

1 cup white button mushrooms (sliced)

½ cup salted dry black olives or Kalamata olives

½ cup chicken broth or water

½ cup wine

- Lightly flour and then sauté chicken in extra virgin olive oil until brown. Set aside
- Chop onion, garlic, and parsley (or use food processor) and sauté in another pan
- Add chicken to sautéed mixture
- Add dried herbs
- Add sliced white button mushrooms
- Add olives
- Add chicken broth (or water) mixed with wine
- Cover pan and cook for 30 minutes

---

## 4) REMOVE CORRECTION FLUID FROM ONE'S HANDS OR THE FURNITURE

Have you ever spilled paper correction fluid on your fingers when correcting a document and then tried to wash it off? Soap and water will simply not work. As much as you try, the stubborn white smudge just won't disappear. To the rescue . . . olive oil. This correction fluid mishap plagued me recently when some of the fluid accidentally got on my six-month-old granddaughter, Christiana, while I was holding her and at the same time correcting a handwritten letter. I quickly massaged her arm with a soft cloth and extra virgin olive oil. Not only did the spots of correction fluid simply disappear, but my granddaughter thought this was all great fun—to be massaged with olive oil by me, her *nonna*. She is a true Italian! This whole process took just a few minutes and, of course, did not harm the baby. Also, if you spill correction fluid on furniture, use the same technique, although you need not use extra virgin olive oil in this instance, just olive oil.

### 5) REMOVE PAINT FROM SKIN

You are right in thinking that my grandparents did not use correction fluid, but they did use paint. Have you ever painted a room in your home or touched up a chip on a doorjamb and accidentally touched the "wet paint" area? If so, you know that it seems as if wet paint has an affinity for skin and often hair. It will appear where and when you least expect it. Olive oil serves as both a lubricant and solvent to remove oil-based paint. To remove paint from hands, skin, or hair, use extra virgin olive oil on a soft cotton cloth. It may take a few minutes, but consider the paint-removal treatment a massage and enjoy.

### 6) DUST FURNITURE

Many of us have heard of the "white-glove treatment," the notion that someone visiting your home will, with her white gloves still on, move her fingers across your furniture looking for signs of dust. It is an old cliché, but I still recall my mother, Gigi (her given name is really Gilda, after the heroine in the opera *Rigoletto*), and her weekly dusting of everything in sight as she prepared for her mother-in-law's visit. My father's mother . . . *Nonna* Rose would "inspect" the house when over for Sunday dinner.

My mother's weekly dusting of furniture was and still is enhanced by using olive oil with white vinegar and water. The vinegar pulls dirt from the wood and that tiny bit of olive oil replaces the oil in the wood. To this day my

mother's wood furniture veritably gleams, and her Sunday
dinners are just as spectacular.

---

*Dusting Formula*

- Mix ¼ cup of white vinegar with 1 teaspoon each of olive oil and water
- Dip your dusting cloth into the olive oil mixture
- Wring the cloth so it is not dripping, and dust
- Repeat as needed

---

And now for a recipe from Gigi's Sunday dinner—
Gigi's Eggplant Parmesan. Because this recipe includes
pesto, I've included details on preparing that as well.

---

*Gigi's Eggplant Parmesan*   (SERVES 6–8)

1 medium/large eggplant
Salt
1 large egg, beaten, plus
   1 tablespoon water (this
   makes the "wash")
1½ cups seasoned bread
   crumbs
¼ cup flour
Pepper
¾ cup extra virgin olive oil

3 cups store-bought
   tomato sauce (e.g.,
   Brother's Mushroom and
   Roasted Garlic, Prego, or
   Paul Newman's)
1 pound mozzarella cheese,
   cut into 12 ¼-inch slices
   (approximately)
12 tablespoons
   Parmesan cheese
6 tablespoons pesto sauce
   (see recipe, page 41)

---

- Trim eggplant; remove tops and bottoms (do not peel); cut into 3/4-inch slices and pierce each slice on each side with a fork
- Sprinkle with salt and leave in colander for a least 1 hour to allow the bitter juices to drain away
- Rinse slices and pat dry with paper toweling
- Mix bread crumbs and flour and pepper to taste
- Dip the slices in the egg wash
- Remove slices of eggplant from the egg wash and coat the eggplant with the bread crumb/flour mix (liberally covering both sides)
- Shake off extra crumbs; pat the remaining bread crumbs until firmly in place
- Heat a generous layer of extra virgin olive oil in a frying pan
- Over medium heat, cook each of the breaded eggplant slices until golden brown
- Place cooked slices on a paper towel to drain excess oil

HOW TO ASSEMBLE

- First, pour tomato sauce to cover the bottom of a large glass baking dish
- Arrange slices of eggplant on the sauce
- Then put one slice of mozzarella on each slice
- Add enough tomato sauce to lightly cover the eggplant and cheese
- Sprinkle on Parmesan cheese
- Dot 1 teaspoon of pesto on top of each slice
- Bake in a preheated oven at 350° for 30 minutes

NOTE: *Eggplant Parmesan may be made ahead, covered, and then frozen. To thaw, place microwave-safe covered dish in the microwave on high for 5 minutes.*

*Pesto*

1 cup fresh basil

2 garlic cloves (peeled)

2 tablespoons pine nuts

2 tablespoons extra virgin
olive oil

¼ cup Parmesan cheese

HOW TO PREPARE

- Place in a food processor the basil leaves, garlic, pine nuts, and extra virgin olive oil
- Blend at high speed for 1 minute
- Add grated Parmesan cheese (enough to make a paste)
- Carefully lift the lid of the blender and scrape the sides of the blender using a small rubber spatula

NOTE: *Store pesto in a jar in the refrigerator (or freezer) until ready to use.*

7)   CLEAN THE AIR AND ILLUMINATE A ROOM

Amazingly, cleaning the air of smoke and pollution is another way to use olive oil. For thousands of years, people have used olive oil with cotton or linen wicks to cleanse the air around them and to keep flames burning for light. In fact, *"Olio come fonte di luce"* (oil as the source of light) is a predominant theme at the Lungarotti Olive Oil Museum in Torgiano, Italy. A beautiful collection of oil lamps, from the pre-classical era to those from the early twentieth century, is displayed. Some of the lamps are decoratively adorned while others are simple and more utilitarian. Crafted from bronze, pewter, marble, iron, terra-cotta, glass, and silver, these olive oil lamps not only cleansed the air but were used as a major source of light for centuries. Even nomads used olive oil lamps for orientation in the desert, and these lamps were considered by some to be inhabited by a benevolent genie.

If you sniff the air above an olive oil lamp, you will smell the pleasing fragrance of the warm oil. Olive oil is 99 percent pure fuel; it does *not* produce smoke or soot, nor does it have an unpleasant odor. People with asthma or chemical sensitivities can burn olive oil lamps without discomfort. Additionally, it is safe; it does not burn if it spills. On the other hand, if burning kerosene is spilled, the fire spreads rapidly. Burning olive oil will smolder and put itself out or give you time to smother it with something. Of course, all flames are potentially dangerous, so keep flames away from children and pets.

Olive oil lamps are commercially available today. I have two. One is called an olive oil chamber lamp and is from Lehman's in Ohio. It is a very practical jarlike lamp with a handle, which makes it easy to move from room to room. The other is a handmade, decorative lamp, which was a gift from my friend Marilee. This lamp is an Elazar olive oil lamp, made of copper and bronze. The woman who makes these unique lamps uses only fire, welding, and water for the patina coloration. Each lamp is unique and quite beautiful. I have referenced these lamps in the Annotated Selected Websites section of the book.

One more bit of advice regarding olive oil lamps. For those of you who think olive oil is an expensive "fuel," it is really quite a reasonable value. The same amount of olive oil that you would use in a salad dressing burns in your lamp for about eight hours. You can also burn the least-expensive olive oil or even one that turned rancid hidden in the back of your cupboard.

Only use an olive oil lamp when burning olive oil. You should not burn olive oil in a kerosene lamp, nor should you burn other types of oil, like petroleum-based fuels or lamp oils, in your olive oil lamp. It is interesting to note that until the 1950s, olive oil lamps were used in Mediterranean towns not yet wired for electricity. Thus illuminating a room as well as cleaning the air are on my list of highly recommended uses for this precious oil.

### 8)  REMOVE TAR SPOTS

Tar spots can really ruin the appearance of a patio or garage. Rubbing an olive oil and baking soda mixture onto the tar spots will take a bit of time, but the results are worth it. Remember my *nonna* Jenny's recipe for cleaning pewter? That same recipe can be used to remove tar spots on concrete or cement.

*Tar Removal Formula*

- Mix ½ cup of olive oil and 2 tablespoons of baking soda
- Dip a dry cloth into the olive oil mixture
- Rub on tar spots, resaturating the cloth as needed, until the spots disappear

## 9) HYDRATE PEARLS AND POLISH DIAMONDS

According to Isabelle Yao, a pearl specialist in Hawaii, the word *hydrate* should really be used in explaining the effect of olive oil on pearls. Put a small amount of olive oil on a soft cloth. Rub the olive oil on the pearls and then lightly buff them with the dry portion of the cloth to remove any dirt and residue and make them shine. Indeed, olive oil will do wonders for all of your precious and semi-precious jewelry. Because I have seen such fabulous results with olive oil on my pearls, I now rub a drop of olive oil onto my diamond jewelry. When my diamond ring catches the sun, its brilliant shine often casts rainbows throughout the room. Your pearls and diamond jewelry can do the same thing.

*Preservation and Prevention*

## 10) PRESERVE WOODEN UTENSILS AND CUTTING BOARDS

In my family, it has always been important to ensure that the life of everyday tools is extended through proper care. I remember watching my grandmothers lovingly preserve all of their wooden utensils and cutting boards. They instilled in me the love for and an appreciation of a well-used kitchen tool. Each and every useful item had a purpose and an intrinsic worth. In my home, I proudly display a very large rolling pin (about forty inches in length). This rolling pin was originally an oar (made out of olive wood) from the time my *bisnonno* (great-grandfather) spent working on a ship in Genoa. In the late 1880s, my *bisnonno* Giovanni was a mariner and traveled the world, often on the seas for more than two years at a time. My great-grandmother died during one of his trips, and his young daughter, my *nonna* Jenny, was sent to America to live with her aunt. Out of one of his ship's oars, Giovanni carved a beautiful, smooth rolling pin, then gave it to my grandmother as a wedding present in 1910. With it, she rolled out the dough for her excellent *sfoglia* (sheets of pasta) for her fabulous ravioli.

Several years ago, after my grandparents died, my mother asked if I would like the rolling pin. Of course, I said yes. And each year when our extended family has our annual ravioli cook-off (our version of a "chili cook-off"), my mother and I use this well-preserved rolling pin to make our favorite ravioli. As I am rolling the crust, I look with wonderment at this historical item, and I continue to use olive oil, as my family has for four generations, to preserve this beautiful wooden utensil.

---

*Spinach and Meat Ravioli*   (FOR ABOUT 200 RAVIOLI)

FOR THE FILLING—THE *RIPIENO*

| | |
|---|---|
| ½ pound spinach (or borage, if you can find it) | ⅓ pound finely ground pork |
| | ⅓ pound finely ground veal |
| ½ chopped yellow onion | 1 tablespoon Italian seasonings |
| 1 chopped clove garlic | |
| 1 tablespoon extra virgin olive oil | 3 large eggs (slightly beaten) |
| | ⅓ cup bread crumbs |
| ⅓ pound finely ground beef | ½ cup Parmesan cheese |

- Wash the spinach (or borage) and cook until soft; squeeze out liquid and mince until very, very fine
- Chop onion and garlic and sauté in olive oil over medium heat
- Add the three types of ground meat and continue sautéing until the meats are brown
- Add the Italian seasoning
- Remove from heat and place in a bowl
- Once the meat has cooled, combine well and add minced spinach
- Add the eggs, bread crumbs, and Parmesan cheese
- Set aside

### FOR THE SHEETS OF PASTA—THE *SFOGLIA*

| | |
|---|---|
| 4 cups flour | 2 teaspoons salt or to taste |
| 1 egg | 1 cup warm water |
| 2 tablespoons extra virgin olive oil | |

### HOW TO PREPARE

- Mix dough ingredients together
- Knead for about 20 minutes
- Press your finger into the dough; if it bounces back, the dough is ready
- Form dough into a ball and cover with a towel or cloth
- Let the dough rest for 30 to 60 minutes
- Divide the dough in half before rolling it out

*Spinach and Meat Ravioli*
Assembling and Cooking

### HOW TO ASSEMBLE

- Roll out two rectangular or square sheets of pasta (equal size)
- On one of the sheets of pasta, distribute olive-sized portions (about ½ teaspoon) of the filling—about 1½ inches apart
- Loosely place the second sheet of pasta on top of the first sheet
- Press down with your fingertips to separate the rows of the filling so that each individual ravioli is formed
- Cut along the rows with a ravioli cutter (wheel)
- Gently press the edges of the ravioli with your fingertips to make sure they are sealed
- Place the ravioli on a lightly floured linen dishcloth, making sure they do not touch

### HOW TO COOK

- Bring lightly salted water to a boil in a large pot
- Delicately place the ravioli in the water
- Cook for 5 to 8 minutes
- The cooked ravioli will rise to the top; however, the only real way to determine if they are cooked (to your satisfaction) is to taste them (the filling should be hot and the pasta cooked through)
- Using a slotted spoon, carefully put the ravioli on a plate and place tomato sauce (see recipe, page 56) on top
- Sprinkle with Parmesan cheese

Most wooden cutting boards in Italy are made from olive wood, and so it is natural to use olive oil to preserve their beauty. The golden liquid can also preserve cutting boards made from other types of wood including oak or maple, and for any and all of your wooden kitchen utensils. Of course, it is important to make sure that the utensils and cutting boards are free from food particles and very clean prior to wiping them with olive oil.

---

*Formula to Preserve Wooden Utensils*

- Hand wash wooden utensils or cutting boards, then towel dry
- Put a small amount of olive oil on a paper or cloth towel
- Very lightly oil the wooden utensils or cutting boards
- You can wash the wooden utensils without worry after oiling, but do not let them soak
- Dry thoroughly after each washing

---

You can lightly rub a lemon wedge on the wood to help keep it free from bacteria, rancidity, and other germs. In addition, once a month or so (depending on use), you may wish to lightly sand the board with a fine-grade sandpaper to keep your wooden cutting board smooth.

### 11)  RESTORE ANTIQUE FURNITURE

I doubt if you will get a hundred-year-old rolling pin, made from an oar, from your great-grandfather, but you may find it useful to know how to preserve your great-grandmother's precious dining room table. Or you may see a fabulous sideboard on *The Antiques Roadshow* and wonder how such pieces maintain their beautiful glow. Here is one of the secrets . . . olive oil. It can remove stains and restore the shine and natural color of the furniture. When applied regularly, the wood will maintain a beautiful luster.

---

*Restore Antique Furniture Formula*

- Mix 1 cup of olive oil and ½ cup of lemon juice in a bowl
- Whisk ingredients together until emulsified and completely blended
- Pour solution into a spray bottle
- Spray onto wood and wipe with a clean, dry cloth

NOTE: *If you wish to make less—it's 2 parts olive oil to 1 part lemon juice*

---

### 12) SAFEGUARD FRYING PANS

Our family life has always been centered around food and the kitchen. However, as I look back, the actual number of cooking utensils we had were few. Today, there are countless kitchen retail stores with voluminous numbers of designer cooking utensils and products. It almost seems that *what* you have to cook with is more important than the final result. If a product or tool doesn't quite meet our culinary expectations, we tend to buy a different one. Not the case in my family. My mother's favorite frying pan, the one that she still uses to sauté onion and zucchini for her famous frittata, is a well-oiled old cast-iron frying pan that was her father's. She claims the frittata always tastes better using that pan. Why? For years, she has treated this pan with love, respect, and olive oil.

You can prevent rust and the loss of luster, as well as enhance a pan's cooking life, by lightly oiling the inside of the pan after each cleaning. Of course, never put these frying pans in a dishwasher. Even though my mother has had a dishwasher for many years, she taught us to hand wash this pan, towel it dry, and then quickly wipe the inside with a small amount of olive oil on a paper towel.

## Firenze's Famous Frittata

1 chopped white onion

2 tablespoons extra virgin olive oil

1 clove garlic

5 medium-sized green zucchini (slice zucchini lengthwise into quarters and then coarsely dice)

5 large eggs (ratio: 1 egg per zucchini)

3/4 cup grated Parmesan cheese

1/2 cup seasoned bread crumbs

Salt, pepper, Italian seasonings to taste

HOW TO PREPARE

- Sauté onion in olive oil; when onions become clear, add garlic and continue to sauté for a minute
- Add zucchini and sauté until zucchini are soft (cover for fast cooking)
- Remove from heat
- In another bowl, beat the eggs
- When zucchini mixture is cool, add to eggs
- Then add the grated Parmesan cheese and bread crumbs and mix
- In oiled frying pan, place zucchini mixture and cook over medium heat until the mixture becomes firm

- When the mixture reaches this stage, your frittata is half finished
- Place a dinner plate over the pan and carefully invert the frittata, letting it slide back into the pan to cook the other side
- When the frittata is golden brown and the egg mixture is congealed, slide onto a plate and serve warm or cold

NOTE: *If you do not wish to try to invert the frittata, you can put it under the broiler in the oven until it is firm and golden in color; or if you travel to Italy, you may find a* girafrittata—*"turn the frittata"—pan for easy flipping.*

---

### 13) PRESERVE KNIVES

Also in the *cucina*, olive oil can be used to preserve knives and to enhance the knife-sharpening process. My mother rarely uses a knife sharpener but rather slides two knife blades together—holding one still and moving the other knife against the blade in a crisscross motion. I am sure she learned this sharpening technique from her mother or father.

Prior to sharpening, my mother hand washes the knives and thoroughly dries them. She then places a small amount of olive oil on a cloth towel and lightly oils the blade of the knives. She then sharpens the knives as described above. I do place my knives in a sharpener, after giving them a light coating of olive oil. This serves two purposes: It preserves the knife from rust or chemical reactions and it oils the sharpener.

While we are on the subject of knives, olive oil will preserve the handle as well as the blade. Put a small amount of olive oil on a cloth towel and lightly oil the black plastic or wooden handle. Notice the shine and luster.

When I attended the Castello della Paneretta cooking school in Tuscany, I noticed that the instructor, Massimo, sharpened his knives in the same crisscross fashion as my mother. His sharp knives chopped, sliced, and diced to perfection while he created many culinary delights, including a fabulous potato and tomato dish. I want to share this great side dish with you:

---

### Massimo's Tomato and Potato Side Dish

| | |
|---|---|
| 4 medium new potatoes | Extra virgin olive oil |
| 6 vine-ripe medium small tomatoes | Peperoncino macinato (crushed red pepper) to taste |
| 1 medium white onion | Salt to taste |
| 2 cloves chopped fresh garlic | |
| 1 sliced lemon | |

HOW TO PREPARE
- Peel and slice potatoes
- Cut each small tomato into four pieces
- Slice onion
- In a pan, layer the potatoes, tomatoes, and onion
- Add garlic
- Douse with extra virgin olive oil
- Add peperoncino
- Salt to taste
- Cook at high heat for 10 minutes
- Lower heat and cook for 25 minutes or until done

---

## 14) PROTECT AND PRESERVE SMALL HAND TOOLS

You can protect metals from chemical reactions, which occur due to the elements in the air that cause rust and deterioration, very simply. A bit of that precious olive oil is all you need to treat clippers, pliers, screwdrivers, scissors, and so on. After using the hand tools, and before putting them away, make sure you clean off any dirt or grime. Put a small amount of olive oil on a cloth towel and lightly oil the tool. You will really notice the difference.

This use of olive oil is centuries old. In fact, the handsaw that my grandfather *Nonno* Vincenzo used to cut the wood material with which he built his home is still in lovely condition. Once a week he would apply a small amount of olive oil to the saw, both the handle and the blade. To this day, my mother has his saw in her garage, and it looks as beautiful now as it did in 1914.

## 15) LUBRICATE GEARS

*Nonno* Vincenzo was also an avid deep-sea fisherman. He would often use olive oil to lubricate the gears on his reel knobs and the swivels on his fishing lure. He probably also used it to lubricate the hooks and even his fishing line, in order to keep it from becoming stiff. He always caught numerous lingcod, a delicious white fish that he prepared beautifully.

## Nonno's Baked Lingcod

1 whole cleaned lingcod
   (head and tail still on, or
   off if you prefer)—
   probably about 20 inches
   in length (but you know
   fishermen)
1 sliced lemon
1 sliced white or yellow
   onion
Extra virgin olive oil

FOR THE SAUCE
One 15-ounce can of Italian
   stewed tomatoes
   (or make your own with
   4 large vine-ripe
   tomatoes, 1 onion,
   1 green or red bell pepper, and 2 cloves of
   sliced garlic)

HOW TO PREPARE

- Open the pocket of the cleaned lingcod
- Insert lemon and onion slices
- Rub the exterior of the fish with extra virgin olive oil
- Place fish in a shallow baking pan
- Spread the tomato sauce on top of fish
- Add ½ cup water
- Bake in preheated oven at 350° for approximately
  30 minutes or until done

NOTE: *You can substitute halibut or salmon or another type
of fish.*

Olive oil can be used to lubricate many items that have
mechanical gears and/or moving parts: the locks on gates,
the rolling parts of toys, sliding tracks for doors, antique
clock pendulums, mouse trap mechanisms, gears on a ro-

tisserie barbecue, blades of a snowblower, car antennas, go-cart gears, well crank handles, gears on an exercise bike, and so forth. When *Nonno* Vincenzo was ninety-six, we even used olive oil for his wheelchair axles.

To keep the precious oil aimed at the exact spot, pour the olive oil into a dispenser with a long spout. Put several drops of the olive oil into the gear mechanisms or the movable parts. Wipe off the excess oil with a piece of cotton or paper cloth.

### 16) POLISH GUNS

My other grandfather, *Nonno* Luigi, was not only a fisherman but a hunter as well. One thing he was very proud of was his gun collection, which he proudly kept polished. He used Nonna's pewter cleaning formula (see page 36) on his guns.

Looking back, I doubt if he ever really shot anything, as he was a very gentle man who loved all types of birds and animals. However, his guns were shiny, and I do recall the culinary delicacy of polenta and quail being served on special occasions. So I guess this gentle man did, from time to time, bring home the quail. And while he was hunting, my *nonna* was making the tomato sauce for the polenta.

## Tomato Sauce for Polenta (or Pasta or Ravioli)

1 medium chopped yellow or
white onion

2 cloves of garlic

Extra virgin olive oil

2 tablespoons chopped
parsley

2 stalks chopped celery

1 medium-sized grated
carrot

1 teaspoon dried
Italian herbs

1 ounce dried porcini
mushrooms

Two 15-ounce cans/jars
stewed tomatoes

Two 8-ounce cans/jars
tomato sauce

HOW TO PREPARE

- Sauté onion and garlic in extra virgin olive oil in a saucepan
- Add parsley, celery, and carrot and continue to sauté
- Add dried herbs
- In another pan, place porcini mushrooms and 1 cup water
  and bring to a boil; turn off the heat and let stand for
  2 minutes
- Drain and chop mushrooms (save the water)
- Add mushrooms to onion mixture and continue to sauté
- In another bowl, drain the stewed tomatoes (saving the
  juice)
- Chop the tomatoes and add to the mixture and continue
  to sauté
- Add the water from the mushrooms and the saved juice
  from the tomatoes
- Add 2 cans of tomato sauce
- Simmer for 1 hour

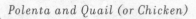

*Polenta and Quail (or Chicken)*

| | |
|---|---|
| 6 quail (or if you don't have quail, use 1 chicken—cut up) | 1 medium onion |
| | Dried Italian herbs to taste |
| | 4 cups water |
| Salt and pepper to taste | 2 cups polenta meal |
| Flour | 1 stick butter |
| 5 teaspoons extra virgin olive oil | Tomato sauce (see page 56) |
| | Grated Parmesan cheese |

HOW TO PREPARE

- Season cleaned quail with salt and pepper and dredge lightly in flour
- Put quail in a frying pan and sauté in olive oil until golden brown; set aside
- In a deep pan, put onion, extra virgin olive oil, and dried Italian herbs; sauté until onions are clear
- Add water; then add polenta, a little at a time, to the mixture and let it come to a boil
- While this mixture is cooking, add the stick of butter
- Keep stirring until polenta is done
- Pour into a glass or ceramic serving dish
- Top the polenta with tomato sauce
- Arrange the quail on top of sauce
- Top with Parmesan cheese and serve

17) PRESERVE BASEBALL MITTS AND
    GIVE BATS GREATER SPRING

The many potential benefits within our ever-present large can of olive oil were certainly not lost on my own son,

Jeff. He has always been sports-minded, and his early training included the cleaning and preservation of his favorite leather baseball mitts—especially during the rainy season. We taught him to clean the mitt of any debris and then, after dripping a small amount of olive oil onto a soft cotton rag, rub the cloth over the entire surface of the mitt. After allowing the oil time to be absorbed, he would then use a dry cotton cloth to wipe off the excess. No need to use extra virgin olive oil for this process—just olive oil.

My son also used this wondrous liquid to oil the surface of his bats à la Joe DiMaggio. In his research, Jeff found that another baseball great, Ted Williams, used olive oil. He would massage the handle of his bat with olive oil and resin in the on-deck circle. The sound that emerged after the bat's olive oil massage would produce a squeal that unsettled many pitchers!

Some people think that olive oil turns rancid too quickly . . . however, for years it has been used to waterproof and preserve porous elements, including wood and leather (as well as skin, but more about that in the next chapter). Try it and see.

### 18) LUBRICATE AND POLISH SKIS, SNOWBOARDS, SKATEBOARDS, AND IN-LINE SKATES

My son is now handing the family olive oil tradition down to his children as he helps them take care of their sports equipment. My grandchildren, especially Evan and Isabella, love to ski, snowboard, skateboard, and skate. Having that handy bottle of olive oil is quite helpful. Olive oil can stop squeaks in ski boots and lubricate the moving parts or gears of both cross-country and downhill skis. To keep sleds and toboggans shined and lubricated for slick movement, use a drop of olive oil.

Olive oil is also a good lubricant for snowboard bindings and for the wheel fittings on skateboards and in-line skates. To keep the gears of this equipment well lubricated, drip the olive oil into the mechanism where the gears move. Remember, only a drop or two is needed. For polishing, use the olive oil and baking soda formula.

## 19) REJUVENATE A PALM OR FERN AND MAKE PLANTS GLISTEN

For years my sister Mary Jill alternated living between Lake Tahoe and Palm Springs. She always had the most beautiful outdoor and indoor plants. In Tahoe, especially in the cold, dry winter months, her trick was to wipe the leaves with olive oil to give them moisture and make them shine. She also moistened the leaves of her plants in the dry Palm Springs climate. One day she told me her secret for her humongous palms and ferns (in fact, she named one of her plants "Hugh"). Once a month she would add 1 teaspoon of olive oil to the soil of a palm or fern. What a way to rejuvenate and feed a plant!

## Repair and Maintenance

## 20) LUBRICATE SQUEAKY HINGES

My childhood aversion to squeaky hinges was reignited several summers ago when a group of friends decided to rent a villa on the outskirts of a small village in Tuscany for a week. Everything about the villa was unique, including the fact that it was owned by two feuding families who had built a wall down the middle and refused to rent the different sides of the villa to each other's friends. It was quite large (even our half) and the views from our hillside location were stunning. When standing on the terraced garden, one could enjoy a 360-degree view of olive trees and vineyards. It was a truly magnificent sight to see the early-morning mist nestled in the valleys. The villa was within walking distance of the small village that included only a church, a small trattoria, and an olive oil mill (*frantoio*). I was told that the entire village is actually owned by a family in Milan, and that the patriarch of the family gave the village and the olive oil *frantoio* to his daughter as a wedding present years ago. (Certainly a different scale of gift-giving than the oar/rolling pin wedding present! However, both stories do involve olive oil.)

Because the village was remote, the nights were extremely still. There were six of us, and we each retired for the night at a different time. Several bedrooms and bathrooms lined the various hallways. Throughout the night, it seemed as if there were never-ending squeaking and creaking noises as people went into and out of their bedrooms and bathrooms. One night one of the men, Mark, unable to sleep because of the shrill squeaks, got up, went into the kitchen, and grabbed the olive oil. With quite a vengeance, he proceeded to oil every single hinge in the villa. We all slept well after that.

To lubricate squeaky hinges, get out your bottle of olive oil and a cloth. Hold the cloth near the squeaky hinge. Put a small amount of olive oil at the top of the hinge and let the drops of oil run down by moving the hinge back and forth. Wipe away the excess with the cloth. No more squeaks! (I don't think Mark carefully wiped each of the villa's hinges, but the floors were tile, so any stray drop of olive oil provided a bit of gloss to the floor.)

You can use this method for the hinges on your oven doors, bird houses, closet doors, tool boxes, plastic coolers, crayfish traps, pruning shears, refrigerator doors, and galley latches.

## 21) POLISH FURNITURE

We stayed for only a week in Tuscany before moving on, and as we were packing, *la signora della pulizia* (the woman who cleaned the villa in preparation for the next guests) started her cleaning. She had numerous rags and bottles with which to clean. She started in the *sala* (living room). She told us that to maintain a deep *lucido* (shine) on the walnut furniture, she used lemon juice, olive oil, and water.

*Furniture Polish Formula*

- In a bowl, mix the juice of one lemon with 1 teaspoon each of olive oil and water
- Dip a clean cloth into the solution and squeeze out excess
- Using a circular motion and following the grain of the wood, apply a thin coat to the wood surface. Let it stand for 5 minutes. Then, using a clean, dry, soft cloth, buff to a deep shine

You can also use olive oil, by itself, to remove water or alcohol spots or stuck paper from polished wood. If paper is stuck to a piece of wood furniture, do not try to scrape it off. Instead, dab some olive oil on the paper. Let the oil soak for a few minutes and then remove the paper by rubbing it with your fingers. What magic!

## 22) POLISH BRASS

The villa had a beautiful chandelier in the *entrata* (entry hall). The large chandelier glistened with a shining brass base and hand-painted ceramic ornaments. I noticed that a trusty bottle of olive oil emerged from the pocketed apron of *la signora della pulizia* as she stood on a ladder to polish the brass. She told me that the brass looks brighter and requires less polishing if rubbed with a cloth moistened with olive oil. Olive oil retards tarnish and helps maintain a shine.

## 23) APPLY TO STUCK ZIPPERS

As we were packing to leave the villa, I wanted to put just one more item in my suitcase but discovered the zipper was stuck. To the rescue—*la signora* and her olive oil. She saw me struggling with the stuck zipper and put a few drops of oil on the zipper, then carefully wiped off any excess oil. The zipper immediately started to move freely. You can use a drop of olive oil on most stuck zippers, including suitcases, makeup kits, wet suits, camping equipment storage bags, and bocce ball or bowling ball bags. However, be *extremely* careful if you ever try to lubricate a stuck zipper on clothes; the oil will stain the fabric around the zipper.

*In a Pinch*

### 24) POLISH LEATHER SHOES

To many, Italy and beautiful shoes are synonymous. While Italy may not be credited with the invention of foot coverings, somehow I imagine the shining and polishing of shoes did begin in Italy and probably involved olive oil. Frequent polishing and shining not only gives shoes a glossy finish, but also preserves their workmanship and quality by moisturizing the leather, thus adding years to their life. Left untreated, leather will dry, crack, and fall apart.

Keeping leather smooth and supple was noted in a 1909 formula, right here in America: "Use Vaseline and olive oil for lubricating dried-out leather." So if you ever run out of your favorite shoe polish, you can use olive oil "in a pinch."

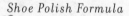

*Shoe Polish Formula*

- Clean dirt from leather shoes using a water-dampened cotton cloth
- Towel dry
- Drip a small amount of olive oil onto a soft cotton cloth and rub over the entire surface of the shoe
- Allow the oil time to be absorbed
- Using a dry cotton cloth, buff the shoes until they shine
- You may wish to apply a small amount of petroleum jelly to a cotton cloth and rebuff the shoes

## 25) SUBSTITUTE FOR LINSEED OIL
## ON SADDLES AND OTHER TACK

Don't we all experience those moments when we don't have just the right product at hand? My granddaughter Victoria is simply wild about horses, and she's learning everything she can about their care. She recently joined an equestrian center for young equine enthusiasts. Every young equestrian at her riding school is responsible for the care of her mount's bridle. After her weekly class, she brings home her horse's bridle to clean it.

One day, not having any of the recommended linseed oil, Victoria followed her *nonna*'s suggestion and used olive oil instead. She wiped off the headstall and the reins and polished them with olive oil. She even wiped off the bit with olive oil, confident that it was healthy for the horse and joking that her horse may even develop a taste for Italian food. When she returned the bridle the next day, she received compliments from her instructor about how supple, clean, and shiny each part was.

## 26) USE AS AUTOMOTIVE TRANSMISSION FLUID—
## EMERGENCY ONLY!

One use for olive oil that has been reported to me, but that I have never tried (and am not recommending), is as a temporary transmission fluid for automobiles. Even in an emergency, I would be very hesitant to put this to the test—since olive oil burns at around 400 degrees, it would be very dangerous over the long haul. But then, what are the odds that you will run out of transmission fluid (on the side of the road) and have a bottle of olive oil in the glove compartment?

## Are You Convinced Yet?

Olive oil provides very simple solutions to many household chores and common everyday problems. Some of the uses you may have already known . . . some are quite novel. Just know that you can keep your entire home running smoothly with my guide to cleaning, preserving, preventing, repairing, and maintaining.

Let me recommend that before you tackle your own personal list of household tasks with olive oil in hand, put on your favorite CD . . . perhaps a bit of "Funiculi, Funicula"; it has great iambic pentameter for doing everyday chores around the house.

Now that your home, and everything inside, is sparkling clean and in the best of condition, let's concentrate on you. Since I was very young, I have always been interested in health—just ask my friends! Staying healthy through natural means is of great importance to me. I love to exercise (sometimes to the annoyance of my friends and family), and I am constantly reading about new ways to stay healthy using natural and easily available ingredients and time-honored folk remedies. In my next chapter, I will share with you information that I have spent nearly a lifetime gathering. Since my school days, I have collected articles and books and magazines on this vitally important topic. As my *nonna* always said, "*Il cibo costa meno delle medicine*"—"Food's cheaper than medi-cine." I have taken that advice to heart—especially con-sidering that my favorite golden oil figures prominently in much of the present-day research on staying in the best of health.

# CHAPTER FOUR

# To Your Health!

WHEN MY GRANDFATHER *Nonno* Vincenzo was ninety-four, he gathered his nine grandchildren together and told us that he wanted to travel to Italy one more time. I was thirty-nine at the time. He told us that he would ask one of us to accompany him. My *nonno* selected me, and for three memorable weeks we visited his sister, my great-aunt *zia* Lena, in a small town on the Italian Riviera. Although I had been to Italy many times, this was the first time that I had the opportunity to spend so much time with my great-aunt and the first time that I realized the myriad health benefits of olive oil.

While spending time one evening around the dinner table talking with my grandfather and his sister, I recalled reading that the Greek philosopher Democritus (circa 400 BC; the law of cause and effect is attributed to him) believed that one could live to be one hundred on a diet of honey and olive oil. While I did not hear a great deal about honey from my grandfather, or from other precentenarian relatives, there were frequent and passionate conversations about olive oil's many health benefits. My relatives would discuss olive oil as a basis for nutritional meals as well as its many other healthful properties and topical uses.

That trip was almost twenty years ago—a time when I wasn't too concerned about free radicals, cholesterol, arthritis, or the risk of colon cancer. Today, as an avid antiaging enthusiast, I have conducted my own extensive research on the topic of aging. I believe olive oil is one of the best nutritional gifts we can give ourselves. Throughout the ages, many folk medicine applications of olive oil have been prescribed. Hippocrates prescribed olive oil for curing ailments over twenty-five hundred years ago.

Olive oil is rich in vitamins A, D, E, and K and contains both omega-3 and omega-6 fatty acids. Recent medical research indicates that olive oil may lower the level of cholesterol in the body and help to prevent coronary heart disease that other oils and fats may actually cause. It may reduce the likelihood of occurrence of certain cancers and can help to maintain a lower blood pressure. It has been known, in some instances, to alleviate arthritic pain. In addition, olive oil stimulates metabolism, promotes digestion, and lubricates delicate mucous membranes.

Olive oil has been a health potion in the Mediterranean area for about four thousand years. As recently as thirty years ago, olive oil, labeled "oleum," was often kept behind the counter at pharmacies, along with morphine, syrup of figs, and kaolin. Speaking of figs, in Algeria, they are often crushed in olive oil and then eaten with the intent of totally cleaning the stomach and the colon. This is an amazingly simple home remedy one could easily try.

Because of olive oil's antioxidant properties, many believe that it can delay the human cell's natural aging process. Among all other edible fats, olive oil is the most digestible and it permits better absorption of vital liposoluable vitamins. In addition, olive oil aids digestion and helps the body absorb calcium. It also contains the necessary amount of linoleic acid, an essential part of the human diet. Linoleic acid is a polyunsaturated fatty acid (of the omega-6 series). It produces a substance (prostaglandin) that is found in every cell and is needed for the body's overall maintenance of good health. It is a fatty acid that must be replenished constantly. What better way to obtain it than from olive oil!

Many folk remedies, used throughout the centuries and covering a wide variety of ailments, do not involve actually ingesting olive oil. These remedies recommend applying olive oil topically, and the uses range from treating ear complaints to killing head lice to relieving jellyfish stings to soothing a sunburn.

Growing up in California and living near the beach, I was actually never stung by a jellyfish, but I often sunbathed. And, as was the custom when I was a teenager, every summer my girlfriends and I would compete for the best tan. Today, I would never go out in the sun without my UVA/UVB sunscreen lotion (SPF 30), but it was much different then! My friends would use baby oil and I would use, what else, olive oil—each of us trying to get the very best and deepest tan possible in the shortest amount of time. Now, we all know it is just not safe to oil up our skin and sunbathe for hours on end. SO PLEASE DO NOT TRY THIS— IT IS NOT ONE OF MY RECOMMENDED USES! What I do recommend, however, is the topical use of olive oil to soothe the dry skin that all too often results after being in the sun for long periods of time. Remember, olive oil contains no sunscreen; *do not* use it for sunbathing.

What follows are some additional health uses—some for the inside of the body and some for the outside; they are a combination of folk remedies and recent medical research. If you are interested in obtaining even more research information, the Internet has a great deal of published data available. Do an advanced search on the Internet to find hundreds, if not thousands, of sites, each able to give you some valuable tips. But it's important to ensure a site is sponsored and maintained by a reliable source. I find that a good starting point for information comes from the California Olive Oil Council (www.cooc.com).

*On the Inside . . . Internal*

### 27) HELP RAISE HDL (GOOD CHOLESTEROL) AND LOWER THE RISK OF HEART DISEASE

Here's an interesting fact: The rate of heart disease is lower in countries where olive oil is consumed daily. Extra virgin olive oil is recognized as being able to lower cholesterol levels in the body. It contains between 60 and 80 percent monounsaturated fats (oleic acid), which helps to reduce the bad cholesterol (LDL) and preserve the good cholesterol (HDL). Raising HDL (high-density lipoprotein) cholesterol is recommended to protect against cardiovascular disease. HDL helps remove the cholesterol that clogs arteries by taking it to the liver for elimination.

To lower your cholesterol, at least 15 percent of your

daily calories should come from monounsaturated fatty acids. Whenever possible, use olive oil in place of butter or other vegetable oils in cooking and/or in the preparation of salad dressings and as a dressing for any cooked vegetables.

---

*Dressing a Salad*

Extra virgin olive oil
Balsamic vinegar
Garlic salt or sea salt
Pepper

HOW TO PREPARE
- Drizzle your best extra virgin olive oil over salad greens and toss (always drizzle the olive oil first and use only enough olive oil to coat each leaf)
- Add a splash of balsamic vinegar
- Season lightly with garlic salt or sea salt and pepper to taste
- An alternative to garlic salt is to slice a garlic clove and toss in the salad (remove the piece of clove—you want just the taste)

NOTE: *You will notice that I did not state the proportions of olive oil to vinegar; when drizzling your best extra virgin olive oil on a salad, just make sure the oil has lightly coated the leaves and then splash balsamic vinegar and add salt and pepper to taste.*

---

28) USE AS AN ANTIOXIDANT

Olive oil is rich in antioxidants, vitamins, and poly-phenols. There are as many as 5 milligrams of antioxidant polyphenols in every 10 grams of olive oil. Polyphenols have been shown to reduce coronary artery disease and may be the substance involved in actually lowering a person's blood pressure. Additionally, antioxidants will reduce nitric acid levels, a substance in the body known to raise blood pressure.

Olive oil contains 1.6 milligrams, or 2.3 IU (International Units), of vitamin E (a natural antioxidant) per tablespoon. One tablespoon provides 8 percent of the RDA (recommended daily allowance) for vitamin E, the vitamin that combats the free radicals that damage body cells and tissues and contribute to aging. Olive oil may be one of the finest substances one can use for delaying the aging process. I feel that it is the best nutritional gift we can give ourselves.

### 29) CALM THE STOMACH AND HELP THE DIGESTIVE TRACT

Unfortunately, today many people suffer from stomach and digestive problems. The use of olive oil has proven to be a beneficial factor in aiding the functioning of the digestive system, and it is believed to have a soothing effect on the stomach. Its other healthful benefits include the reduction of stomach acid, which can be a cause of stomach ulcers.

---

*Calm the Stomach*

- Upon rising and before eating anything: Take 1 tablespoon of extra virgin olive oil to stimulate digestion

---

The same remedy can be used to prevent flatulence and heartburn. As you read on, you will see that I refer to this "1 tablespoon upon rising" throughout the book. Just know that taking *only 1 tablespoon* is necessary to enjoy the benefits I outline; no need to take more, unless you want to!

### 30) USE AS A NATURAL LAXATIVE

Another positive effect olive oil can have on the digestive system is that it reduces the chance of constipation by aiding in the passage of food through the digestive track and bowel. The mild vegetable mucilage in olive oil protects the body's digestive tract and acts as a natural laxative. Take extra virgin olive oil alone; if you don't like the taste (I can't imagine that!), you may wish to mix it with lemon juice.

---

*Natural Laxative*

- Take 1 teaspoon of extra virgin olive oil mixed with the juice of a medium-sized lemon on an empty stomach

---

### 31) AID IN PREVENTING GALLSTONES

Gallstones, a very painful malady, are hard, round lumps of solid material usually composed of bile or cholesterol. Olive oil stimulates bile secretion and regulates the emptying of the gallbladder, which may help to prevent gallstones. Recent studies do show that olive oil has a very positive effect on the gallbladder and that the incidence of gallstones is relatively low among people who live in areas where olive oil consumption is high.

There is a well-known "gallbladder/liver flush" remedy that uses olive oil along with apple juice, epsom salts, and lemon juice. The process is quite involved; for more information, see *The Amazing Liver Cleanse* by Andreas Moritz. However, always check first with a medical doctor if you think you have gallstones, and always get medical advice prior to considering a liver cleanse.

### 32) EASE THE PAIN OF ARTHRITIS AND BURSITIS

Bursitis and arthritis can afflict a person with a great deal of pain, swelling, and stiffening, and it can severely reduce one's range of motion. One tablespoon of olive oil, taken one half hour before breakfast, is reputed to help ease these symptoms and may even reduce the development of these two chronic illnesses. According to a Greek study (published in the *American Journal of Clinical Nutrition*, December 1999), consuming extra virgin olive oil reduces the risk of rheumatoid arthritis. A quote from this study states: "Those with the lowest lifetime consumption of extra virgin olive oil had a 2½ times greater chance of developing rheumatoid arthritis than those with the highest." In addition to swallowing that daily morning tablespoon of extra virgin olive oil, put some on your hands and massage the affected areas. This, too, may ease the pain of arthritis and bursitis.

### 33) AID IN THE PREVENTION OF COLON CANCER

Numerous studies point to the fact that olive oil may aid in the prevention of colon cancer. According to the

National Cancer Institute (American Cancer Society. *Cancer Facts and Figures*—1997, Atlanta, Ga., 1999) more than 75 percent of colon cancer cases could be prevented by diet. An Oxford University study found that "olive oil, perhaps through its influence on secondary bile acid patterns in the colon, appears to protect against the development of colorectal cancer." The study published in the *Journal of Epidemiology and Community Health* (October 2000), included participants from twenty-eight countries, including the United States. Research data showed "new evidence of olive oil's protective effect on colonic mucosa" and concluded that individuals consuming large quantities of olive oil have a lower rate of colon cancer.

### 34) RELIEVE COLDS, SORE THROATS, AND COUGHS

When winter arrives, colds, sore throats, and coughs usually follow. The winter months on the Italian Riviera, where my relatives live, are very cold and damp and can be quite severe—especially in my *zia* Lena's home, which did not have central heating. She told me how she often warded off colds (and probably other people!) with her olive oil and crushed garlic formulas. I prefer a sweeter version.

*Sore Throat or Cough Remedy*

- In a pan, mix 3 to 4 tablespoons of lemon juice, 1 cup of honey, and ½ cup extra virgin olive oil
- Warm for 5 minutes over low heat on top of the stove
- Take 1 tablespoon every two hours

My friend Joanna lived in Rome for many years, and while there she thoroughly enjoyed the good life we all associate with living in that magical city. She would often eat out, and in Rome, eating out with friends *always* involves drinking wine. She shared with me her secret for reducing the effects of alcohol. She told me always to take 2 teaspoons of olive oil before going out on the town and drinking. The olive oil prevents alcohol from entering your bloodstream so quickly. "It acts like a cork to the stomach," Joanna told me. This tip was verified by the *Global Hangover Guide*, which also suggests swallowing two spoonfuls of olive oil before drinking. This guide rather humorously notes: "But that leaves all the alcohol you drank for naught (if getting drunk is, in fact, your objective)."

*On the Outside . . . External*

### 36) TREAT EAR COMPLAINTS

Whenever I mention my passionate interest in the uses of olive oil to my friends or relatives, they invariably tell me, "My mother used to put warm olive oil in my ears when I was a child to help with earaches." This natural oil soothes the pain.

Olive oil can be used to clear "stopped-up" ears or for painful earaches. To clear ears, put a few drops of warm virgin olive oil in the affected ear. Lie down for a few minutes, affected ear upward and with your head on a terry-cloth towel, then turn over so that the olive oil can seep out onto the towel. Or you can use a favorite remedy from *Nonna* Jenny—the garlic oil ear remedy.

---

*Garlic Oil Ear Remedy*

- Crush a couple of garlic cloves into some virgin olive oil or olive oil
- Let it sit for several hours at room temperature then strain
- Keep the oil in the refrigerator and warm just a little of it as needed
- Put a few drops of the warm garlic olive oil in the ear canal
- Plug the ear loosely with a piece of cotton
- This mixture will keep in the refrigerator for one week

---

A caution: Never put anything liquid in your ear if you think there is any chance at all that you may have a perforated eardrum or any other serious medical condition, and never ever treat a child or infant without medical advice. Check with your doctor or pediatrician immediately!

### 37) USE FOR A SOOTHING ENEMA

What a subject . . . but one that is sometimes necessary to discuss. Assuming that there is no underlying medical condition, an olive oil enema may help soothe the intestinal lining, and it can also be useful in the overall cleansing of the colon. An important caution: If you have a gastrointestinal condition, such as irritable bowel syndrome (IBS), Crohn's disease, ulcerative colitis, or any other chronic intestinal tract disorder, do not attempt this remedy except on the advice of your physician. In any acute situation, where pain is significant or is accompanied by fever, redness, or swelling, or where appendicitis is suspected for any reason, you should call a doctor immediately.

---

*An Olive Oil Enema*

- Pour into an enema bag 1 cup of extra virgin or virgin olive oil and 1 cup of organic aloe vera juice
  Or
- Try an enema made from 5 ounces of olive oil and 20 ounces of boiled water (cooled to lukewarm)
- Slowly insert into the rectum
- Hold for 3 minutes; then eliminate

---

### 38) KILL HEAD LICE

It is hard to think about olive oil and head lice in the same sentence. However, olive oil is the main ingredient in a well-accepted program for this all-too-common problem. In the United States, lice attack more than 12 million people a year. Head lice are easily transmitted from person to person through direct contact—by the sharing of combs, brushes, hats/caps, and linens. While the most commonly prescribed treatments for head lice are pediculicidal shampoos and cream rinses, these products contain harsh insecticides. A more effective and safer way to eliminate head lice is through the Head Lice to Dead Lice Treatment Program, a treatment that uses olive oil to smother and kill active head lice. Entomologists at the Harvard School of Public Health have confirmed the safety and effectiveness of this treatment, which consists of a series of olive oil treatments applied to smother chemically resistant lice. The treatments are timed specifically to disrupt their life cycle. If you would like more information on using olive oil in this way, visit www.headliceinfo.com.

### 39) SOOTHE FROSTBITE

Frostbite, which is defined as the freezing of the skin and the underlying tissues, can be very dangerous and should be attended to as soon as possible. Caused by long exposure to icy air and freezing winds, frostbite interrupts circulation to affected areas. If medical attention is not immediately available, you may wish to begin the following folk remedy while on your way to the doctor (or hospital). Start by exposing the frostbitten area to warmth (not heat), and then apply the following soothing frostbite remedy.

---

*Soothing Frostbite Remedy, aka the "Camp Pack"*

• Mix 1 ounce each of olive oil, peppermint oil, and ammonia
• Gently rub on the frostbitten area

---

This is such an effective treatment that you may want to keep it handy when hiking or camping. Okay, how many of you take olive oil, ammonia, and peppermint with you camping, hiking, or skiing? Next time you head out into the great outdoors, make certain that you include a "camp pack" of the above mixture just in case!

## 40) TREAT CUTS, BLISTERS, AND SUNBURNS

My grandmother *nonna* Jenny taught us to put olive oil on a cut. I still today reach for the small bottle of olive oil I keep in my medicine cabinet for small cuts and abrasions. I use olive oil instead of other over-the-counter products.

For painful sunburns, use olive oil to help soothe the reddened skin and even the blisters that sometimes follow too much sun exposure. Remember, olive oil is *not* intended to be used as a suntan oil, primarily because it does not contain any sunscreen, but it can be of great help after one has experienced a sunburn.

---

*After-Sunburn Olive Oil Remedy*

- Mix extra virgin olive oil with an equal amount of water
- Beat until it becomes an emulsion (like mayonnaise)
- Apply to the affected area
- For blisters, make a compress of warm olive oil and chamomile tea
- Apply to the blistered area

---

## 41) SOOTHE DRY OR CHAPPED SKIN

A side effect of winter weather, besides the aforementioned colds and sore throats, can be dry and chapped skin. This condition can become quite a painful problem, causing cracking and even bleeding of the affected area. To provide quick relief to one's skin, make a simple emulsion of water and olive oil, and then apply it to the dry, chapped area. The emulsion can really alleviate this problem.

Another way to use olive oil is to soften dry or rough elbows. The following olive oil ointment is another of those indispensable family formulas:

---

### Olive Oil Ointment

- Mix 1 pint of virgin olive oil or olive oil with 1½ ounces of beeswax
- Slowly heat until melted
- When cool, apply to the dry or chapped skin area
- To store the excess, place in covered jar and keep in a cool place

NOTE: *You may wish to add 2 to 3 drops of your favorite essential oil*

---

### 42) RELIEVE MUSCLE CRAMPING

Muscle cramping, a stiffening of the muscles into a painful spasm, usually experienced after exertion, is an all-too-common problem for many of us. It's caused by a buildup of acid in the muscles. An application of olive oil mixed with clove oil can help relieve cramping. Include a small bottle of this potion in your gym bag for immediate relief after a prolonged workout.

> *Muscle-Cramping Relief Formula*
>
> - Mix equal amounts of virgin olive oil or olive oil and clove oil
> - To relieve a cramp, dip a towel in hot water, squeeze, and place it over the affected area for a few minutes
> - Then remove the towel and massage the oil mixture into the heated muscle

### 43) REPEL INSECTS

This is an extremely useful bit of information, particularly if one lives in an area inhabited by mosquitoes and other flying/biting insects. Did you know that mosquitoes are less likely to bite skin that is covered with olive oil? Happily, it's true!

### 44) SUFFOCATE A TICK

Although we usually associate the pesky problem of ticks with our pets (and this is addressed in greater detail in the chapter on pet care), ticks can plague humans as well. Whether visiting a beautiful wooded area or living in a lovely countryside location, children (and adults) come into contact with ticks, which attach themselves aggressively to the skin and resemble soft black bumps. Not only are they an irritation to one's skin, some ticks can carry Lyme disease, a serious health problem, so it is very important to get rid of ticks as soon as you spot them. I suggest trying this "tick trick" and see how a simple application of olive oil—what else?—will cause the tick to back away from the point of entry. Here's what to do. If the tick has been attached to the skin for an hour or less, try smothering the pest by dripping olive oil on it. Leave the olive oil on for 10 to 15 minutes, and the tick may actually back out. A doctor friend of mine just tried this "tick trick" on his daughter. To his amazement, it worked, and quite quickly. Of course, if the tick does not back out or if it has been attached to the skin for more than two hours, seek medical attention.

### 45) RELIEVE JELLYFISH OR MAN-OF-WAR STINGS

If you are ever unfortunate enough to be bitten or stung by a jellyfish or man-of-war, apply olive oil from your trusty "camp pack." You should also seek immediate medical attention since jellyfish bites and stings can be very painful and lead to other problems.

Now that we have learned how olive oil can contribute to one's health, both internally and externally, I would like to share with you some of my family's "secret formulas" for using the magical golden liquid in beauty treatments. Read on.

# CHAPTER FIVE

# Beauty Is Skin Deep

FOR CENTURIES, people of the Mediterranean have recognized the beautifying benefits of olive oil for the body, skin, and hair. In fact, the *first* uses of olive oil were actually *on* the body and not *in* it. In ancient Egypt, Rome, and Greece, olive oil was infused with herbs and fragrant grasses to produce cosmetics as well as medicines.

Researchers continue to find proof of the healing and beautifying attributes of olive oil. In fact, not long ago, archaeologists at a Mycenae excavation site uncovered a list enumerating different ointments composed of olive oil and various aromatics, such as fennel, rose, sage, and watercress. Even the ancient Indian holistic technique Ayurveda suggests using olive oil and water to bring skin to its maximum hydration and beauty.

For generations, my family has passed along time-honored recipes for potions, elixirs, and beauty masks.

For literally thousands of years, Italian women have used olive oil in daily beauty rituals. From the top of their heads to the soles of their feet, olive oil has been *the* source of many beauty treatments. Even Renaissance writer Isabella Cortese, in her *Secreti* books, touted "the secret" uses of olive oil as a natural beautification remedy. Our family, too, has always prided itself on having smooth skin and shining hair—aided by—what else?—olive oil! In this chapter, I will share with you some of our family's beauty secrets. As my father used to say, *"Everything old is new once again."* Or was that Cole Porter or Peter Allen?

Olive oil is indeed a beauty oil. In addition to its other properties, the oil helps to improve the appearance and texture of one's skin and hair. Need proof? I have heard of three great beauties who regularly use olive oil in their beauty regimens and are happy to share their secrets with the world. If you know who Jane Seymour is, then you know how amazingly beautiful her long hair is. She attributes its shine and overall radiance to regular olive oil treatments. Then there is the forever-lovely Sophia Loren. I've read that this beautiful woman takes two tablespoons of olive oil every day. A third famous beauty, Juliette Binoche, follows her hairstylist's recommendation that she use a hydrating shampoo and conditioner made with olive oil. Certainly we can all agree on the positive results these three women have achieved!

On the subject of hair, before electric clippers came to barbershops throughout Italy, barbers used a drop of olive oil to maintain the moving parts of the hand clipper's blades. If a bit of the precious oil dripped on the hair . . .

no problem. The gentleman left the shop with a sharp new trim and shining hair to boot.

When I think of all the wonderful, alluringly packaged beauty products, whose list of ingredients include an infusion of olive oil, I often think of my father's cousin Louisa. Louisa had two passions in her life: her family and her special beauty regimen. To care for her beautiful skin, she would exfoliate it with olive oil and salt. To condition her long dark hair, she would regularly apply a conditioner of the precious oil.

When my sisters and I were young, we were amazed that this older woman had such shiny hair and smooth and supple skin, and we were, I must admit, a bit amused by her ways. I imagine she envisioned herself as an ancient Roman goddess as she took particular care with her "sacred" beauty rituals. When she died recently, at eighty-eight, she still had the most beautiful skin and hair. In her honor, I have included Louisa's beauty formulas in this guide.

Today's beauty-conscious adults are looking to spas for the latest in beauty treatments; spas are perceived as *the* sources of the secrets to eternal youth and beauty. People the world over are sparing no expense in their pursuit of the very latest beauty craze, and it's no surprise to me that many top spas include olive oil treatments as a part of their many exotic offerings.

While attending the annual Sonoma Olive Festival this past year, I noticed that several spas and hotels featured special Olive Festival Packages. The package at one hotel included a one-hour herbal wrap with a warm olive oil massage. The olive oil was infused with mandarin orange, cinnamon, and bergamot. There was also mention of olive oil pedicures—recommended for those with "beauty-challenged feet."

Among all the natural lipids, olive oil has the chemical distribution most similar to human sebum (for non-biology majors, sebum is the body's own natural skin lubricant). This similarity gives olive oil a strong affinity to human skin. Olive oil is completely safe, easily absorbed, and has a "cell-refattening" capacity. By making a simple emulsion (by mixing equal parts water and olive oil), a perfect balance between water and oil is produced—as water rehydrates the skin and olive oil protects it from delipidification (losing its own natural lubrication).

More and more aromatherapists and massage therapists are using olive oil as a base for their oils and potions. A "warm olive oil massage" offered at fine hotels and spas points to the documented health- and beauty-enhancing benefits of olive oil.

Many of the beauty tips that follow, while not scientifically proven, have been handed down in my family for generations. Unless otherwise noted, use an early-harvest extra virgin olive oil (the greener the better) for each of the beauty applications. Olive oil is natural and pure, and the greener oils tend to have more antioxidants and less greasy characteristics. I have also read that the best extra virgin olive oil for the skin is from cultivars that have the highest percentage of polyphenols (antioxidants) and alpha tocopherols (vitamin E). For example, try Coratina, Cornicabra, Koroneiki, Moraiolo, and Picual.

*For the Skin*

### 46) DISCOVER *THE* ULTIMATE BEAUTY SECRET

Interested in having skin like a fashion model? Many models and others in the fashion industry attribute the perfection of their skin to the swallowing of at least 1 tablespoon of extra virgin olive oil each morning. You can follow their advice in one of two ways: first thing in the morning, either swallow 1 tablespoon of straight extra virgin olive oil or combine ½ cup warm water, 1 tablespoon of extra virgin olive oil, and 1 tablespoon of apple cider vinegar in a glass and drink the mixture. I love the taste of straight extra virgin olive oil and actually savor its flavor. It may take a while for you to find your favorite olive oil—yes, tastes of oils vary just as the tastes of wines and other things do. In the chapter on Parties and Special Occasions, I give some tips for throwing an olive oil–tasting party—you and your friends will enjoy this one!

But, getting back to the recipe, some people prefer the apple cider vinegar and olive oil mixture because the vinegar purportedly acts to remove toxins from one's system, while the olive oil lubricates the inside of the body. However, when the oil is mixed with apple cider vinegar, make sure to drink it quickly. *Talk about an acquired taste!*

---

*THE Ultimate Beauty Secret*

• Upon rising and before eating anything, swallow 1 tablespoon of extra virgin olive oil

Or,

- Mix ½ cup warm water, 1 tablespoon of extra virgin olive oil, and 1 tablespoon apple cider vinegar
- Drink quickly!

---

## 47) REJUVENATE DRY SKIN

Extra virgin olive oils make wonderful moisturizers for both the face and body. A key benefit of these completely natural moisturizers is that you do not have to worry about any of the potentially harmful or allergenic ingredients found in some commercially prepared creams and moisturizers available today.

I use olive oil on my face (and body) straight out of the bottle; however, my cousin Louisa whipped up her own custom moisturizer, utilizing various ingredients straight from her kitchen. Her favorite moisturizing formula included Italian parsley (she said it was an antibiotic that also combated "lurking germs"), water (to release parsley's benefits), and olive oil (to lock in the moisture).

---

### Louisa's Moisturizing Formula

- Combine 1 teaspoon of finely chopped fresh Italian parsley with 1 teaspoon of hot water
- Add 1 tablespoon of extra virgin olive oil
- Mix well
- Moisten your face with warm water
- Apply the mixture to your face with your fingers in an upward circular motion

- Leave on for 5 minutes
- Remove by blotting with a soft cloth
- Make sure the parsley is blotted away!

At night, apply the oil mixture more heavily and leave it on till morning for a deep-rejuvenating beauty treatment. You may wish to leave out the parsley. I do not use olive oil as a moisturizer directly under makeup because I find that it makes my makeup run. If you do use it under makeup, make sure you have blotted your skin and removed any excess oil (and parsley!) before following up with your makeup application.

### 48) SMOOTH OUT WRINKLES

Olive oil both softens and smoothes the skin, leaving it very supple. It has exceptional penetrating ability, and is able to lock natural moisture in, thus preventing dry skin. In addition, it is high in well-documented antioxidant properties. Olive oil has the natural ability to target epidermal keratinocytes (the basic cells from which the upper layer of skin is made) and can stimulate the synthesis of collagen and elastin, thus encouraging firmer and healthier skin. There are some excellent commercially prepared olive oil creams, or you can make your very own beauty creams.

*Nighttime Antiwrinkle Formula*

- Mix 1 tablespoon of extra virgin olive oil and several drops of the juice of a lemon

- Apply the mixture to the face (except around the eyes and eyelids)
- Only apply straight extra virgin olive oil to the under eye and eyelid areas
- Keep on overnight

### 49) EXFOLIATE WITH AN OLIVE OIL SALT GLOW

Do you ever find your skin in a dry and flaky state? It can be so disheartening! But once again, our magical golden oil can come to your immediate aid. It's so simple to have beautifully smooth and glowing skin all year round with the regular use of a completely natural exfoliator. Use an olive oil body scrub, and your skin will feel smooth instantly. My cousin Louisa did, and her skin remained beautiful her entire life.

Extra virgin olive oil has its own great scent and, used alone or in combination with sweet-smelling drops of lavender or geranium oil, will leave your skin smooth as well as fragrant.

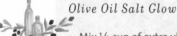

*Olive Oil Salt Glow*

- Mix ½ cup of extra virgin olive oil with 1 tablespoon of coarse-grained sea salt
- Add drops of lavender and/or the essential oil of geranium (optional)
- Massage the body
- Shower afterward

Make this formula right before using it; store any extra in a plastic or glass container for later applications. I find it easier to make it just before massaging on my body or on someone else's body . . . oops, those details are in a different chapter!

## 50) MASSAGE FEET

Good news for those of us on our feet for long periods of time: Olive oil can relieve and revive tired feet. Olive oil has excellent emollient and moisturizing properties, and massaging the feet with olive oil will help with cracked heels. You can give yourself a foot massage, or, better yet, get someone else to give you a foot massage (and then return the favor). For a relaxing foot massage, use olive oil foot massage remedy #1.

---

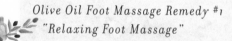

*Olive Oil Foot Massage Remedy #1*
*"Relaxing Foot Massage"*

- Mix in a small bowl
  2 teaspoons extra virgin or virgin olive oil
  3 drops lavender essential oil
  1 drop chamomile essential oil, and
  1 drop geranium essential oil
- Wash the feet thoroughly and adopt a comfortable position
- Rub the mixture all over each foot with a rotating motion
- Put on socks after massage to absorb the excess oil

---

For a foot-awakening or revitalization foot massage, use olive oil foot massage remedy #2. The combination of olive oil with sea salt, fresh peppermint, and lemon zest will make your weary feet stand up and take notice.

---

*Olive Oil Foot Massage Remedy #2*
*"Reawakening Foot Massage"*

- Mix in a small bowl
  2 teaspoons extra virgin or virgin olive oil
  1 teaspoon sea salt
  1 drop peppermint oil, and
  ½ teaspoon lemon zest
- Wash the feet thoroughly and adopt a comfortable position
- Rub the mixture all over each foot with a rotating motion
- Rinse the feet and apply straight olive oil
- Put on socks after massage to absorb the excess oil

---

51) MASSAGE THE BODY

The basic goal of massage is to help the body heal itself and increase health and well-being. Massage improves circulation, increases blood flow, and brings oxygen to body tissues. For an olive oil massage, start with extra virgin or virgin olive oil as your base, then add rosemary oil for relaxation or mint oil for stimulation of muscles.

---

*Olive Oil Massage*

- Mix in a small bowl
  8 ounces extra virgin or virgin olive oil
  ¼ ounce rosemary oil

---

or

⅕ ounce mint oil
- Rub the mixture all over the body

You will find additional massage formulas and techniques in the chapter on Olive Oil and Sensuality.

### 52) SOAP YOUR ENTIRE BODY

Olive oil soap is a natural cleansing and moisturizing beauty soap. Because of its emollient and soothing effect, it softens and moisturizes the skin and hair as it cleanses. It is also gentle enough for most types of sensitive skin. Fortunately, there are many commercial olive oil soaps currently available in specialty shops and markets, like the remarkable Savon de Marseille, which, according to a 1688 French law, is made using specific ancient methods and the purest ingredients. Although you can use a lower grade of olive oil, my friends who make their own soap prefer to use extra virgin olive oil in their soap-making efforts. Olive oil is made into soap by the addition of lye; colors, fragrances, and additional moisturizers, such as glycerin, can be added as well. To me, the whole process of soap making seems to be quite complex, with special safety issues surrounding working with lye. I have been told, "If you can cook, you can make soap." However, I prefer to *buy* my olive oil soap. If you are a soap maker and wish to find out more, check Annotated Selected Websites in the back of the book. I have also included the names of specialty stores where olive oil soap is sold.

## 53) REMOVE EYE MAKEUP

Extra virgin olive oil is so pure and nonirritating that you can safely use it around your eyes to remove makeup. You need use only a small amount of extra virgin olive oil for eye makeup removal.

Pour a very small amount of oil onto a clean cotton pad and gently wipe over your eyelashes and eyelids. Or you can pour a small amount in one hand and, with the fingers of your other hand, smooth the oil over your eyes and eyelids. Then use a clean cotton pad or soft tissue to remove all traces of makeup. Not only will all of your eye makeup be completely gone, the delicate skin on your eyelids will be moisturized and glowing.

## 54) USE IT AS A FACIAL MASK

Getting ready for a special night out? Want your skin to positively *glow*? A simple face mask made of olive oil and mashed avocados is easy to make and apply, and just wait until you see the final results! Your friends will simply marvel. All you need is extra virgin olive oil and a ripe avocado.

*Olive Oil and Avocado Face Mask*

- Use ½ cup of extra virgin olive oil
- Mash 1 small ripe avocado
- Mix together to smooth consistency
- Apply to the face
- Leave on for 12 minutes
- Rinse off and see how great your skin looks

I learned another face mask formula from Patrizia, my cooking teacher in Tuscany. Patrizia not only cooks with olive oil, but she also uses it on her face. Her formula substitutes clay (available in health food stores) for the avocado. It is called Mascher di Argilla—face mask of clay.

---

*Face Mask of Clay*

- Mix 2 tablespoons fine clay with 1 tablespoon extra virgin olive oil
- Add enough water to make a smooth consistency
- Apply to the face
- Leave on for 15 to 20 minutes
- Rinse off, dry, and apply moisturizer

---

## 55) SOOTHE SENSITIVE SKIN
### AFTER WAX TREATMENTS

With fashion's ever more revealing clothing, a bikini wax has become one of life's inevitable beauty treatments. And although the end result is worth it, this beauty treatment can leave one's skin red and irritated—our ever-present bottle of extra virgin olive oil to the rescue! Use olive oil to remove excess wax and/or to soothe the area of skin that has been waxed.

To remove excess wax, dab on a little extra virgin olive oil and, using a soft tissue or cotton ball, gently rub the newly waxed area in small circles. To soothe after waxing, pat the affected areas with an olive oil–soaked cotton pad. If your aesthetician is not yet aware of this soothing treatment, make sure you bring your own flask of olive oil. Let the oil be absorbed by the skin so as not to leave a VOOP (visible olive oil line).

Of course, extra virgin olive oil can be used following other waxing treatments, including the eyebrows, legs, back, and so forth.

### 56) SHAVE WITH IT

There are many, many shaving foams, gels, and other types of softening and moisturizing products on the market—for both women and men. Ever stand confused in that aisle at the drugstore? Do not be confused any longer. That's right, along with all of its other beauty tricks, olive oil can be used to soften one's beard, or other "hairy parts," prior to shaving. I think that olive oil is much better overall than other commercially available creams for the skin, and it can soothe accidental nicks during the shaving process. So next time, before you buy another shaving product, try using extra virgin olive oil. Follow the same procedure you would use with a commercial shaving cream. You will experience an amazingly close and smooth shave.

While we're on the subject of shaving, shaved heads are popular today. If you or a friend happen to be fond of this look, here's a tip: Use extra virgin olive oil; it will gently lubricate this sensitive area of the body. My personal hairstylist, Michael (voted the number one hairstylist in Los Gatos, California), also teaches shaving classes. Here are his tips for a clean shave of the head . . . or wherever:

## Michael's Professional Shaving Instructions

- Make sure you clip off hair using a professional groomer or clippers (especially in preparation for shaving of the head or if you have a beard)
- Heat the area to be shaved with a damp, hot towel
- Lather the area with extra virgin or virgin olive oil and let it sit for a few minutes
- Using a disposable razor or a wet/dry electric razor, carefully shave going with the grain of the hair; keep dabbing the area with water
- You may wish to reapply the olive oil and very carefully reshave the area in the opposite direction
- Michael suggests taking a shower after shaving—to rinse any nicks
- Put a cold towel on the shaved area
- Pat dry
- Apply a toner or aftershave lotion or balm

NOTE: *Michael advises that you use a disposable razor only once, and that if you use a wet/dry electric shaver, make sure to follow the cleaning instructions to inhibit the growth of bacteria.*

If you have an extra special day (or evening) when you want the smoothest and closest shave possible, Michael suggests that you let your beard or head hair grow for two or three days and then follow the professional shaving instructions.

Michael also gives other advice. Before shaving your legs, try the olive oil salt glow formula (page 94). Exfoliating your legs before shaving makes for a sleek, smooth shave.

### 57) REJUVENATE YOUR LIPS

Winter or summer, olive oil can be used as a lip balm to soothe chapped and dry lips. What girl wants to kiss or be kissed with dry lips?! Never one to waste a ripe banana (and how much banana bread can you really eat?), my mother taught me this special formula.

---

*Lip-Rejuvenation Formula*

- Use ½ ripe banana and 2 tablespoons of extra virgin olive oil
- Whip together to make a smooth paste
- Apply to your lips
- Leave on for 20 minutes
- Rinse off and see how great your lips look and feel

---

*For the Hair*

### 58) CONDITION DRY HAIR

Here is yet another amazing beauty recipe (once again from my now-almost-famous cousin Louisa)—this one will make your hair the envy of all of your friends. Olive oil does two things to the hair; it increases its strength as well as improving its overall flexibility. This is especially important if you regularly use hair dryers and heated rollers—both of which can be very drying to the hair.

---

*Olive Oil Hair Conditioner*

- Mix ½ cup virgin olive oil or olive oil with an egg yolk
- Add a few drops of lemon juice and mix
- Then shampoo your hair with your favorite gentle shampoo and rinse
- Apply the mixture of olive oil, egg, and lemon all over your hair
- Leave on for 5 minutes
- Shampoo your hair again and rinse
- Shampoo, once again, to completely remove all residual olive oil and rinse

---

### 59) MAKE A WARM-OIL TREATMENT FOR THE HAIR

If your hair is extremely dry and brittle, you may wish to use a warm-oil treatment for an intensive conditioning. Even if your hair is not dry, giving it a warm-oil treatment once every three months will prevent the onset of dryness.

---

*Warm Olive Oil Treatment*

- Pour ¼ cup virgin olive oil or olive oil in a blender, then carefully add ¼ cup boiling water (be careful!)
- Blend at high speed until the oil and water have emulsified
- When the mixture is warm, massage it into your hair

- Warm your oiled hair with a hair dryer for a few minutes
- Wrap your hair in a thick terry-cloth towel for 15 minutes
- Remove the towel and shampoo with a small amount of your favorite shampoo
- Rinse and shampoo again to completely remove all residual olive oil

### The Really Quick Warm Olive Oil Treatment

- Warm ¼ cup of virgin olive oil or olive oil in the microwave
- Making sure that the oil is warm, not hot, carefully pour over your head
- Massage into the scalp for several minutes and run your fingers through the length of your hair to completely saturate
- Then shampoo with a small amount of your favorite shampoo
- Rinse and shampoo again to completely remove all residual olive oil

You may wish to leave the oil on your hair overnight. If you do, use an older pillowcase while you sleep to protect your bedding; olive oil can stain. See page 212 for some tips on removing olive oil stains.

### 60) TREAT DANDRUFF AND HAIR LOSS (WELL, MAYBE)

Much to the dismay of men (and some women), hair loss seems to affect many in the world today. Olive oil may actually *prevent* hair loss. Although there are no guarantees (everyone is different), I suggest that you give this family formula a try to see if the treatment will work for you. We know it will prevent dandruff (because of olive oil's effect on dryness) and it may, hopefully, slow or even prevent hair loss. This wasn't the case for my dear *nonno* Vincenzo, who happened to be as bald as a bocce ball, but he did not have any dandruff.

---

### Dandruff and Hair Loss Prevention

- Massage your scalp with extra virgin olive oil every evening for 8 days leaving the oil in overnight. (This will allow it to work its way completely into the scalp)
- Shampoo in the morning to remove all residual olive oil

NOTE: *Remember to use an older pillowcase and remember the tips to remove olive oil stains.*

---

### 61) CONTROL FRIZZ AND CREATE SHINE

An annoying problem with overly treated hair is an all-too-common condition known as "the frizzies," and I'm certain that we have all experienced them at one time or another. To the rescue once again is my favorite potion—olive oil. Just a drop of virgin olive oil applied to wet or dry hair can control frizz and create a truly enviable shine. Remember to put only a very small amount (a drop or two) of virgin olive oil or olive oil in the palm of your hand; then rub your hands together and finger comb through your hair.

### 62) IMPROVE THE APPEARANCE
### OF NAILS AND CUTICLES

Throughout history, well-manicured nails were a symbol of refinement, culture, and civilization—distinguishing the commoner from the aristocrat. Olive oil applied to one's nails and cuticles will create a healthy glow and generally improve the overall appearance of both fingernails and cuticles. The following olive oil treatment is based on an old Egyptian recipe, possibly even from Cleopatra, who certainly knew how to take care of her body, her kingdom, and also her nails.

---

*Nail and Cuticle Treatment*

- Mix together 1 tablespoon of extra virgin olive oil, 1 teaspoon of honey, and 1½ teaspoons of sea salt
- Massage a small amount into your nails and cuticles
- Wipe off any excess with a clean cloth and lightly buff
- End the treatment with a few drops of olive oil massaged onto your hands

---

### 63) STRENGTHEN NAILS

Use olive oil in the treatment of dry and brittle nails; it helps to moisturize them and will restore their flexibility and strength. Soak your fingernails and toenails in warm water and then in warm olive oil for five minutes. This sequence will soften the cuticles and help brittle nails become more resilient. You can remove the excess oil with a clean cloth and massage the remainder into your hands.

## 64) SOFTEN HANDS

Have you ever noticed that the best chefs have the most beautiful hands (and cuticles)? I have been told that it is because they use olive oil so often in food preparation. So let's go back to the kitchen (this time not just to make polenta) to solve the beauty problem of dry hands.

*Polenta-Style Hand Softener*

- Combine ¼ cup of cornmeal and ¼ cup of extra virgin olive oil
- Mix into a paste
- Massage the cornmeal paste into your hands
- Rinse
- Put a small amount (a drop) of olive oil onto your hands and massage

As we leave the chapter on beauty and continue on to the discussion of the many sensual uses of olive oil, I once again think of Louisa, who, during her life, probably never traveled more than about 250 miles from her home. She would never have understood my lifestyle. For fifteen years, my job as an international business management consultant had me on the road 100 percent of my work time. Each Monday morning I would fly to a client site, stay at a local hotel for four nights, and fly back home on Friday. With limited suitcase space available in my ever-trusty carry-on bag, I was forced to carefully consider what I could take with me on the road. So, to handle my many personal grooming tasks, I would remember Louisa and include a small plastic bottle filled with extra virgin olive oil. Although olive oil is best stored in glass, for traveling, plastic is easier, safer, and lighter. I always put the bottle in a sealed plastic bag away from my packed clothes. Then, upon my arrival, I would use the packed extra virgin olive oil in a variety of ways.

First thing in the morning, I would swallow 1 tablespoon of extra virgin olive oil (remember the story about Sophia Loren?); at night, I would remove my makeup with olive oil, and then, after washing my face, I would apply the olive oil (with a bit of water) as a nighttime moisturizer. If my nails and cuticles were overly dry from all the air travel (we all know how drying the inside of an airplane can be!), I would give my hands a quick massage; if I needed to shave my legs, I would use the olive oil as shaving lotion; and, if my shoes looked dull, I would moisten the shoe cloth with olive oil and give them a quick polish. I would then be ready for my next client appointment—perfectly groomed and feeling great, inside and out.

Now that every part of your body, from the very top of your head to the bottom of your feet, is smooth, supple, and soft, what better time to read about the many uses of olive oil in more, shall we say, "companionable pursuits." My next chapter includes formulas and solutions (made from olive oil, naturally!) used to massage, tantalize, and otherwise appeal to our amorous and romantic partners. After all, isn't one of the primary points of beauty to attract that very special someone? It is certainly one of beauty's (inside and out) benefits in my humble opinion, and my many Italian relatives concur. Read on!

# CHAPTER SIX

# Olive Oil and Sensuality

THE HISTORY OF using olive oil in the sensual and erotic arts is as old as olive oil itself, dating back to the early Greeks—and continuing through many other cultures well known for their sexuality, such as the Romans.

Historians have written about the sexual practices of the early Greeks and Romans and the various types of pleasure-enhancing devices used in their erotic pursuits. Evidently, these early lovers actually lubricated their devices with the sacred oil of the olive. You, too, can re-create the ancient art of giving of pleasure through touch—enhanced through the use of olive oil. Read on and perhaps a new fantasy, involving the use of this ancient and sacred oil, will lead to that illusive and mystical glow that has long illuminated stories, folklore, and legends in our Western history.

Sexuality (and sensuality) is a key component to a person's general well-being. Scientists have long studied human sexuality, and recent research finds that vitamin E can actually improve one's sex life. Good news! Olive oil is rich in this marvelous vitamin. While we cannot truthfully say that olive oil by itself is an aphrodisiac, the olive and its oil have been considered important to both fertility and fruitfulness; in ancient times and throughout history, Greek women often slept on olive leaves when they wished to become pregnant. The olive tree was considered to be a tree of fertility. Eating olives and using olive oil is purported to increase fertility, lust, and sexual potency in men. My advice, ladies, serve olives often! And gentlemen, enjoy your daily dose of olives!

Olives add a delicious flavor to that martini. They are great in salads, on pizzas, or by themselves. The olive's rich and unctuous flesh adds sensuality to any dish. You can find them pitted, sliced, or puréed into an olive paste (like a tapenade).

---

### Olive Paste or Paste di Olive

2 cups pitted, cured olives
   (Taggiasca or Kalamata)
1 sprig fresh rosemary
Pinch of fresh thyme

1 teaspoon anchovy paste
3 tablespoons extra virgin
   olive oil

HOW TO PREPARE

- Make sure all olives are pitted
- In a blender or food processor, mix the rosemary and thyme (you may use a mortar and pestle in this step)
- Add the olives (or olive pieces)

- Blend thoroughly until the mixture forms an olive paste
- Remove from blender and place mixture into a bowl
- Stir in the anchovy paste
- Add the extra virgin olive oil a teaspoon at a time keeping the olive paste more on the "dry" side

HOW TO SERVE
- Serve with small toasted dry crostini,
  or
- Add a small amount of cream when serving with pasta,
  or
- Add to dough when making focaccia

---

Fertility was critical to the very survival of early people—both through abundant harvests and the continual births of healthy babies. Being one of the first oils, olive oil was widely used by the priests and priestesses of yore to ensure both human fertility and abundant agricultural harvests. In this ancient and magical world of sacred rituals, designed to honor the gods and goddesses, olive oil was a key component of many important ceremonies and rituals, including fire rituals, first for burning and later used to coat sacred candles. Many ancient formulas for special ritual oils call for the use of olive oil as the fixative or base. Olive oil is still used today as base oil when mixing herbs for essential oil blends.

Try a special potion made with extra virgin olive oil. One can infuse olive oil with a special fragrance or "essence" and use it as a magical potion of attraction. Use extra virgin olive oil as the base oil and then add other essential oils to make Love Oil, described by Scott Cunningham (author of books on natural magic and herbs) in his book *Magical Aromatherapy.*

---

*Love Infusion Formula*

- Place ⅛ cup extra virgin olive oil (as a base oil) in a glass container
- Add the following essential oils and turn the container clockwise after adding each oil:
  6 drops of ylang-ylang (a soothing scent, creating desire)
  3 drops of palmarosa (a compelling citrus scent)
  3 drops of lavender (a scent long associated with spiritual and romantic love—it even is claimed to calm untamed lions)
  2 drops of geranium (a rich green roselike scent that both calms and refreshes at the same time)
- Use in the bath (about 10 drops) or dilute with another ¼ cup olive oil for massage
- Just a note: It is best to make this oil just before using it; essential oils tend to oxidize rapidly when mixed with the base oil and may cause the base oil to become rancid, if kept for more than a couple of months

---

Now, for more information on the subject of massage. Oils are a most vital ingredient in massage; you rub some onto your hands and then place them in contact with the skin of the person you are massaging. A fine oil will keep your hands free from any friction and thus ensure a pleasurable experience for both the person being massaged as well as the masseuse. You need only a small amount of my favorite golden liquid to give a loving massage and well lubricate your partner's skin. Olive oil tends to be more viscous and a bit sticker than vegetable oils, and it absorbs into the skin much better than either mineral or baby oils. Just imagine the combination of enjoying a meal rich with olives and olive oil and *then* giving or receiving an olive oil–infused bath or massage—ah, can lust be far behind?!

You can (and should!) lavish olive oil onto your partner with great joy and delight. In your massaging enthusiasm, be careful not to spill oil on the sheets or the floor. I find that filling a plastic, flip-top bottle keeps the process neater. Oil placed in a dish or in a bottle with a screw top can spill much more easily. (Then again, who cares . . . sometimes it is just easier to grab a bottle of olive oil.)

Warm the oil before applying it to your partner's skin; cold oil can be a shock. Either warm it in your hands or put the bottle into a bowl of warm water. Pour the warmed oil onto your hands first and then rub it on your partner's body. Slowly drizzling the oil from the bottle can tickle a bit—but maybe that is exactly the effect you want! Keep a small hand towel nearby to remove the excess oil, if you'd like, or just let it drip away with great abandon!

Below are just a few ideas I have included to spark your imagination and arouse your innate sensuality. While this is not a gourmet's guide to sensual pleasure, what follows can definitely spice up your love life—through the highly enjoyable application of this ancient, magical, edible, lickable oil. Do let me know of your experiences. . . .

### 65) BATHE IN IT

Water is the most therapeutic of all elements; its buoyancy can invariably lift your spirits. Add olive oil, and water's all-over embrace gives freedom to both your body and mind. So take this "bathe in it" idea any way you want. Just a note of caution, before you read on—olive oil will make any surface slippery, so watch your step!

I recommend frequent soaks in oil-enriched water. You can pour the extra virgin olive oil straight out of the bottle directly onto the body and then submerge yourself into the warm water and leisurely bathe; afterward, hop (carefully) out of the bath and into a nice steamy hot shower and loofa the excess oil off your skin—as it washes down the drain, just feel your cares slip away. Your entire body will feel alive and oh so soft. Wrap yourself in a plush terry-cloth towel and head for your bed with a good book, or perhaps with some other pleasurable pursuit in mind. There is just nothing that feels so good!

Or you can go for another type of fully enjoyable and re-laxing experience, either alone or with a partner. Make the mood extra romantic and luxurious by lighting several care-fully selected candles and scenting the room with their sen-sual essential oils. Have your extra virgin olive oil close by.

For the *ultimate* "bathe in it" experience, you will need olive oil, lavender oil (or your favorite cologne), candles, sweetly scented flower petals, some favorite champagne, and very romantic music.

---

*The Ultimate "Bathe in It" Experience*

- Turn on your favorite music
- Pour ¼ to ½ cup (depending on tub size) of extra virgin olive oil into very warm bath water

- Fill the tub as high as you are able (considering that two of you will be in the bath)
- Add several drops of lavender oil or other aromatic oil (or you can use your favorite cologne or perfume)
- Light the candles
- Float fragrant flower petals
- Call your sweetie into the bath
- Luxuriate in the experience
- For many reasons, use care when stepping out of the bath

---

You may wish to take a brisk, cold shower for a tingling feeling of all-over vitality after your bath . . . or you may just wish that this relaxed feeling would go on and on and on. . . .

There are many things one can add to this wonderful ritual. Feel free to make it your very own and incorporate it into your regular lovemaking practice. Consider adding a face mask of avocado with olive oil. Lick it off your partner, or use a massage glove to gently (or, not so gently, with olive oil and salt) oil your body or your partner's body. Make something up and write to me, and I'll include it in my next book.

---

*The Not-So-Gentle Olive Oil Salt Massage*

- Mix ½ cup extra virgin olive oil with 1 tablespoon coarse-grained sea salt
- Add drops of lavender and/or the essential oil of geranium (optional)

- Massage the body
- Shower and proceed . . .

---

## 66) DRIZZLE IT ON . . . THE BODY

The cooking chapter advises drizzling extra virgin olive oil over vegetables, salads, and meats. This drizzling of oil over great food provides texture and taste and ultimately adds to everyone's optimum enjoyment of a beautifully and carefully prepared meal. So, if drizzling olive oil can work magic with wonderful food, just think of how drizzling olive oil onto the skin could add to the enjoyment of time spent with a romantic partner.

Let's get back to our discussion of the sensual uses of olive oil. As we have previously read, using olive oil for sensual massage is a centuries-old delight. If one is going to "drizzle it on . . ." this practice is optimally done with a partner. Once again, extra virgin is the best type to use on skin. Use the amount necessary depending on body size, the actual part of the body being massaged, and degree of fun intended. Here are some ideas for massage, but by all means feel free to experiment.

---

*The "Drizzle It On . . ." Experience*

- Spread an old sheet across a bed or floor
- Turn on your favorite music
- Serve a light Italian wine in your most beautiful wine goblets

- Have a plate of finger foods at hand (see suggestions below)
- Light candles (even in daylight, they always enhance a romantic and pleasurable moment)
- Take out your warmed bottle of extra virgin olive oil and prepare to drizzle away on neck, shoulders, ears, and head
- Legs
- All four cheeks!
- Back
- Hands and feet
  and
- Time permitting, the whole body would benefit from this loving application of oil from the gods

---

This experience could prove to be most memorable, and one that you will want to replicate on a regular basis. Time spent with a dear loved one is sacred time, and studies have shown that it is good for your entire being. So don't rush! Take your time and keep that bottle of olive oil always ready!

Prepare some easy finger food ahead of time—such as grapes, cheese, and focaccia. My *nonna* used to spend hours in the kitchen making her focaccia (we called it *fûgassa* in our Genovese dialect) in her woodstove. Not to worry, though, I have found a much easier way to prepare it. (I doubt if my *nonna* would have used a prepared dough *or* put her recipe in the sensuality chapter of a book on the uses of olive oil.) But I thought many readers might turn to this chapter first, and I wanted to make sure that each of you learns this very easy recipe (it always receives rave reviews whenever I have served it at a dinner party or just as "finger food").

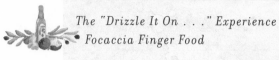

*The "Drizzle It On . . ." Experience*
*Focaccia Finger Food*

| | |
|---|---|
| 1 loaf of Bridgeford Bread Dough (they come 3 to a package) | Sliced onion—use about ¼ of a medium-sized onion |
| Extra virgin olive oil | Garlic salt or coarse sea salt |

HOW TO PREPARE

- Place 1 frozen bread loaf on a well-oiled, large baking pan (or use the bottom of your oven baking pan)
- Drizzle extra virgin olive oil on top of the frozen loaf
- As the bread dough thaws, flatten the loaf out with your hands several times adding a bit more olive oil
- When the bread dough is completely thawed (about 3 hours), smooth it out to the edge of the pan and make fingerprint "wells" in the dough
- Place thinly sliced white onion on the top of the dough
- Sprinkle lightly with garlic salt or coarse sea salt
- Cook at 350° for about 20 minutes
- Remove from oven and immediately drizzle more extra virgin olive oil on the top and brush the oil over the entire surface
- Let it cool for a few minutes and cut into squares
ENJOY!

Always taste the focaccia so that the salty side touches your tongue first; this activates your taste buds. Use the oil from this delicious finger food, which may linger on your hands, to continue massaging your own hands or your partner's.

I am endeavoring to maintain a "respectable" presence in the olive oil industry, so I shall rely on your creative imagination to "fill in the blanks" in this particular section. My historical research indicates that throughout the ages olive oil has been deemed an excellent sexual lubricant. There are, however, a couple of caveats associated with this particular use of the oil: First, do not use olive oil as a contraceptive or put it on condoms. Oil causes latex to break down, resulting in holes and tears. Second, people may experience irritation. According to all the doctors I have contacted, olive oil is completely natural, and, if it doesn't cause any problems for you or for your partner, go ahead and use it with pleasure. Also, compared to other oils and lubricants, olive oil has a very appealing flavor, which can further enhance a sensual encounter.

A closing thought—olive oil can stain. If it does get on fabrics, take the items to your dry cleaner. Using the tips on page 212, you will often be able to wash oil out of bed linens.

And one more closing thought—if you happen to be in a hotel and have forgotten to pack your travel-sized bottle of olive oil . . . just call room service and order a salad with double extra virgin olive oil *on the side.* It will work splendidly, you won't have to leave the room, and no one will be the wiser.

What better chapter to follow this one than Pregnancy and Baby Care. A couple will often be able to recall that their baby was conceived after a wonderfully romantic night spent together. Naturally, my big Italian family is always overjoyed at the news of an impending birth, and members immediately begin to offer all of their individual advice and old family remedies for anything and everything that a new mother and father might encounter. So, let's see how we can use olive oil for the family.

# CHAPTER SEVEN

# Pregnancy and Baby Care with Olive Oil

ONE OF THE MOST exciting and busiest times in a family is the arrival of a new baby. Part of the prearrival preparation in my family was passing down information regarding the care of both new mother and infant. Naturally, many of my family's historical solutions to the problems of pregnancy and infancy centered on that most magical of potions—what else!—olive oil.

Many pregnant women and new mothers consider olive oil an absolute mainstay to help them in the care of their babies. Extra virgin olive oil is healthful and has a natural composition that is particularly good for pregnant women, infants, and young children.

Good nutrition is key to having a problem-free pregnancy and a healthy baby. There are many different schools of thought regarding the special nutritional requirements of a pregnant and/or nursing mother. However, a good starting point, and one about which there is little dispute, is that extra virgin olive oil is good for pregnant women, especially with its high content of vitamin E.

In addition to vitamins and other minor components, olive oil is composed mainly of fatty acids, including approximately 73 percent oleic acid, 9 percent linoleic acid, and 0.3 percent linolenic acid. Remember (from the health chapter), linoleic acid is that fatty acid that must be replenished constantly. It is a polyunsaturated fatty acid (from the omega-6 series) that produces the substance that is found in every cell and is needed for the body's overall maintenance of good health. Oleic acid is the fat that is mainly present in a human being's body, as opposed to the fat found in the bodies of other mammals. Most amazingly, extra virgin olive oil has a similar composition to the fats found in maternal milk.

So convinced are they of olive oil's innate health properties, people from the Mediterranean area for centuries have spoon-fed it to children (starting at around five months old); they consider it a good growth supplement for infants. Olive oil contains vitamin A and, along with its high percentage of oleic acid, is reported to stimulate bone growth and encourage the absorption of calcium and minerals. It also helps with gastritis, a problem that plagues many infants and young children. Nature's natural remedy, extra virgin olive oil, to the rescue! It acts to coat the delicate stomach lining of the baby or young child. Of course, always check with your pediatrician for answers to questions or advice on your baby's health.

Externally, olive oil is so mild that it is often recommended to keep a baby's sensitive skin soft and moisturized. It protects the skin from drying and, because it is a natural substance, there is no fear of chemical reactions. Olive oil is also good for a baby's hair. A friend told me this "old wives tale": When he was quite young, his Italian grandmother shaved his head and massaged it with olive oil. She promised that this practice ensured a lifetime of good and healthy hair. He is now a seventy-six-year-old bambino with a beautiful head of hair.

Another friend, Eileen, shared with me her home-birthing experience, in which olive oil played a major role. Her midwife told her to massage (actually, to have her husband massage) her perineum with olive oil during her pregnancy and to make sure that she had a bottle of unopened olive oil with her birth supplies (unopened so that it was free of contamination). During the birthing process, the midwife generously applied olive oil to the perineum in order for the area to stretch and become more pliable and, I guess, for the baby to "slide out." Eileen delivered her ten-pound daughter, Rachel, without requiring any stitches—no tears! She did tell me that Rachel came out "smelling like a sumptuous salad" and that, to this day, her daughter "loves Italian food." After hearing this story, I researched the practice and discovered the ancient method of using olive oil in birthing is key in home-birth deliveries today.

I was not delivered at home, but my lifelong passion with olive oil began quite early, when I was a baby, although I wasn't consciously aware of it at the time. As was the custom when I was born, my dear mother nursed me— and my two sisters. I didn't realize until I was much older and heard her speaking with her close friends that she had a special secret "solution" to take care of herself while she nursed us. She mixed olive oil and water to make an emulsion, which she put on her breasts to soothe the tender tissue that was sore from the feeding process. For years, she shared with her friends the secret of this very soothing emulsion.

While this breast-soothing practice is not common here in the United States, it is one of the first uses that comes to mind when Italian women are asked how they use olive oil, other than for cooking. "Put it on the breasts, when nursing," they quickly exclaim. What follows are just a few special uses for mommy and baby. Check the health and beauty chapters of this book for additional ideas.

*For Mommy*

### 68) ALLEVIATE AND LESSEN THE APPEARANCE OF STRETCH MARKS

A young mother has much to look forward to with the birth of her new baby. Along with many good things come a few things that are not so positive—I am thinking here of stretch marks. Many women the world over suffer from this problem during their pregnancy. In fact, over 90 percent of all pregnant women will get stretch marks.

The good news is that for most women these unwanted marks will fade after pregnancy. How prone one is to getting stretch marks has a great deal to do with both individual skin type and genetics. While preventing them is difficult, here is an anti–stretch mark formula that will not only soothe a new mother's ever expanding skin, but, according to some women, lessen their appearance, when applied daily.

---

*Anti—Stretch Mark Formula*

- Apply a mixture of equal parts warm extra virgin olive oil and pure cocoa butter on the stomach, buttocks, and breast areas

---

Another tip to try in the battle to lessen the appearance of stretch marks is mixing a small amount of extra virgin olive oil with a small amount of self-tanning lotion. Apply this mixture directly to the stretch marks, and they will be less noticeable.

### 69) SOOTHE NIPPLES WHEN BREAST-FEEDING

And now, back to the time-honored formula to take care of cracked, sore, and chafed nipples. Prior to nursing, always moisten your nipples with water. Then immediately after nursing, apply the following formula.

---

*Formula for Soothing Nipples*

- Whip equal amounts of extra virgin olive and water to make an emulsion
- Gently apply to breasts to soothe and treat cracked nipples immediately after nursing your baby

---

If rose water is available, you can substitute rose water for the plain water and mix it with equal amounts of extra virgin olive oil. I suggest extra virgin olive oil because you want mommy and baby to have the very best in terms of quality and taste.

*For Baby*

### 70) SOOTHE BABY'S DIAPER RASH

Every new mother has faced the pesky problem of diaper rash. What to do to ease this very painful problem? Olive oil, of course! Extra virgin olive oil is good for cracked and chafed skin, including a baby's diaper rash. This old family remedy is a truly magical ointment, and it's very easy to prepare. Of course, always ask your pediatrician prior to using any formula on your baby.

---

*Diaper Rash Remedy*

- Mix 2 teaspoons of extra virgin olive oil with 1 teaspoon of water
- Whip the water and olive oil together until you create an emulsion
- Spread it on the baby's bottom

---

An alternative remedy, which is a bit more complex, is to add calendula flowers to olive oil.

## Diaper Rash Remedy with Calendula

- Put 1 cup extra virgin olive oil and a handful of calendula flowers into a heavy glass jar and shake
- Place the jar in a hot water bath
- Reduce the heat and simmer for 1 to 2 hours
- Strain the calendula out of the oil using a strainer lined with cheesecloth
- Apply the strained oil directly to the baby's bottom

NOTE: *Put a pan of water on top of the stove, and bring the water to a slow boil.*

## 71) ALLEVIATE BABY'S CRADLE CAP

Cradle cap is a form of *Seborrheic dermatitis* (a type of dandruff), often seen in newborn infants. Your baby may just have a mild case of dry, flaky skin (that looks like dandruff), or he may have a more severe case marked by thick, oily, yellow patches. Throughout the years, there have been many home remedies for cradle cap.

One of the most noted of home remedies for alleviating a baby's cradle cap is massaging olive oil directly onto the affected scalp area.

## Cradle Cap Remedy

- Gently massage your baby's scalp with extra virgin olive oil (with your fingers, a soft baby brush, or a soft washcloth)

- Leave it on for at least 10 minutes
- Then wash and rinse the baby's entire head with warm water
- Take special care with the "soft spot"

---

## 72) MAKE YOUR OWN NATURALLY SAFE BABY WIPES

For the past twenty-five years, baby wipes have become a mainstay on each and every changing table. A mother can actually make her very own, natural baby wipes, which will be very gentle for a baby's tender skin. They are also excellent for anyone with extremely sensitive skin.

---

*Baby Wipe Formula*

- Mix the following:
  2 cups warm water
  2 tablespoons baby shampoo, and
  2 tablespoons extra virgin olive oil
- Soak heavy, soft, white paper towels in the solution
- Squeeze out extra moisture and fold moistened towels
- Store in an empty baby wipe container or plastic bag

---

## 73) GIVE YOUR BABY A HEALTHY, INVIGORATING MASSAGE WITH OLIVE OIL

If you have never given your new baby a massage, you have missed a really great treat. Human touch not only helps an infant to bond with a parent, but also builds trust between mother, father, and baby. Both you and the new baby will benefit from the time spent in this wonderful pursuit. Just watch your baby giggle and coo with enjoyment when you give him a little massage.

---

### Baby Massage Tips

- Rub the extra virgin olive oil into your hands to reduce the friction on the baby's skin
- Make sure that the room is warm, since your baby will be wearing only a diaper
- Use gliding strokes or circular motions and press ever so gently
- Don't forget the baby's fingers and toes, and take special care if you massage the baby's head (you may wish to avoid that "soft spot")

---

Infant massage is best performed with the use of gentle, extra virgin olive oil. It will lubricate your hands as well as soothe your baby's skin. In fact, in "Oil Versus No Oil Massage," a study done by Touch Research Institute and published in *Perinatology*, infants showed fewer stress behaviors (e.g., grimacing and clenched fists) and lower cortisol levels (stress hormones) following massage with oil versus massage without oil. Of course, natural oils—like extra virgin olive oil!—are preferred over mineral-based oils.

Further studies conducted at the Touch Research Institute found that babies who receive regular massages are more alert and even cry less than those who do not receive massages. So massage away!

### 74) MOISTURIZE BABY'S NOSTRILS

Here's another problem that can be treated easily. During the dry winter months, or when traveling by air, everyone's nostrils can become a little bit dry, and a baby's extrasensitive nostrils can become especially dry. To alleviate this problem, just put a small amount of extra virgin olive oil on the end of a cotton swab and carefully swab the baby's nostrils.

Now that we've covered the care of both mother and baby through the use of olive oil, it's time to turn our attention to the other "babies" who may share your home—dear pets. Dogs, cats, and other furry friends are important members of today's homes. These loving creatures look to us for their care, and pet owners go to great lengths to provide for the health and happiness of their pets. Many of my friends have generously shared their olive oil feeding, health maintenance, and grooming care tips with me. In the next chapter I will share that useful information with you.

# CHAPTER EIGHT

# The Care and Feeding of Your Pets with Olive Oil

ALL OF MY animal-lover friends have shared with me stories of how they use olive oil in the care and feeding of their pets. Just like their human companions, pets can also reap the health benefits of olive oil. It is good for their heart, reduces bad cholesterol, and keeps their skin and coat glossy! A friend gives her basset hounds 1 tablespoon of olive oil, once a day, drizzled on their food. The oil works to prevent dry skin—from the inside out. Also, this daily application of olive oil dramatically improves the shine of their coats, and it apparently even makes their food taste better—just ask Watson, one of my favorite dogs, who is CBO (chief basset officer) of his own company, Watson's Marketplace (www.watsonsmarketplace.com). He has his own special dinner and liver-cookie recipes that include olive oil! (See page 140).

Rosie, my cousin's border collie, had a terrible problem with fleas, and she scratched herself until her skin was raw. My cousin was at her wit's end trying to help her beloved dog. Someone suggested that using a bit of olive oil to soothe the area might just bring some relief to Rosie's suffering. Rosie herself seemed quite happy with the suggestion. She not only got relief from the itchy fleabites, but she really loved the flavor of the olive oil. Rosie was a great taste tester for this remedy, and it proved to be the solution to her problem. My cousin was thrilled! I also told my cousin (and Rosie) that ticks, those surface-dwelling parasites that attach their mouths to a part of the skin and will not move, can actually be smothered by using olive oil.

Getting back to Watson, his human companion, Ellen, is involved with Basset Rescue—a nationwide service to help place abandoned basset hounds. Her rescued bassets often come to her with bruises and scrapes, evidence of past mistreatment or neglect. She uses a variety of oils on their skin and coats to cure many of their ailments, and olive oil is one of them, because it is natural and nontoxic and we know dogs will lick almost anything off their coats. Ellen even oils her dogs' collars with olive oil so that they will remain supple and not chafe canine necks.

Another use that Ellen makes of olive oil is in the care of her dogs' footpads. Think of walking barefoot across hot sand (à la Dudley Moore in the film *10*). Imagine walking barefoot in the snow or on hot pavement. Weather extremes (too hot or too cold) can hurt tender feet—whether human or canine. Applying olive oil can soothe your pet's paws, as evidenced by Ellen's well-tended dogs—there's nary a cracked paw pad among her pack of bassets.

Remember, the same conditions that plague humans have also plagued our pets for centuries. For other ideas, please refer back to the many recipes, formulas, and solutions found in the health and beauty chapters. For example, when reading the health chapter, keep in mind that vitamins A, D, E, and K and omega-3 and omega-6 fatty acids are also good for your pets. They can reap the same benefits, from alleviating arthritic pain to promoting digestion. And when reading the chapter on beauty, you may follow (for example) the same formula and procedure for your pets that you do for keeping your nails strong and cuticles moist. Give your pet a "peticure." And remember, while this chapter deals mostly with dogs and cats, these uses for olive oil can be adapted to other animals as well.

## On the Inside . . . Internal

### 75) SHINE YOUR PET'S COAT AND KEEP YOUR PET HEALTHY

Olive oil is wonderful oil that, when added to your pet's favorite food on a regular basis, can help to maintain a beautiful, shining coat. In addition, supplementing your pet's food with this marvelous oil maintains good lubrication of their bowels. This is especially important if your pet gets only dry food for its regular diet.

Here are Watson's favorite recipes, generously provided by his owner, Ellen:

### Watson's Dinner Recipe

3 ounces raw ground turkey
3 ounces cooked brown and
   white rice
4 ounces vegetables

1 tablespoon oat bran
¼ teaspoon powdered
   vitamin C

**HOW TO PREPARE**

- Mix the ingredients and feed to your favorite canine
- In addition, once a day, give your dog one 200 IU vitamin E,
  1 tablespoon (for medium-sized dogs) of extra virgin olive
  oil (alternate with fish oil), and one multivitamin

### Watson's Liver Cookies Recipe

12 ounces oat flour
12 ounces rolled oats
3 teaspoons bouillon
   granules (or 3 bouillon
   cubes)

2 eggs
1 cup cold water
1 pound liver puréed in the
   food processor
¼ cup extra virgin olive oil

**HOW TO PREPARE**

- Preheat oven to 350°.
- Mix ingredients and pour into a 13 × 9-inch greased pan
- Bake for 1 hour; let pan cool and then cut contents into
  squares
- Serve during walks or as treats anytime
- If you freeze the cookies, they will last up to 6 months

My veterinarian suggests using liver from organically raised animals for the above recipe. He also recommends what he calls his Coat Conditioning Mix, which includes a combination of animal, vegetable, and fruit oils for coats that need that extra TLC. You should begin to see a difference in about three weeks.

## Coat Conditioning Mix

1 cup extra virgin olive oil
1 cup safflower oil
1 tablespoon cod liver oil

**HOW TO PREPARE**
- Mix together and drizzle on your dog's food, but do not overwhelm the flavor of the food
- The amount varies based upon the size of your dog (See serving instructions below.)
- This mixture can keep for up to one month in the refrigerator

## Serving-Size Instructions

Remember to use your judgment for serving size of straight extra virgin olive oil or the Coat Conditioning Mix. For small dogs, weighing up to 20 pounds, use ½ teaspoon;

for medium-sized dogs, weighing up to 50 pounds, use 1 teaspoon; for larger dogs, weighing up to 100 pounds, use 1 to 2 tablespoon(s); for extra large dogs, use up to ¼ cup.

### 76) SLOW THE SHEDDING PROCESS

Shedding occurs in all pets—dogs, cats, birds, reptiles, or hamsters. It is natural and an all-too-common problem, and one with which olive oil can help. Whenever your pet is shedding excessively, try adding extra virgin olive oil to her food, keeping in mind the serving-size instructions above. You will notice that the shedding process will slow . . . less hair on couches, floors, and chairs to vacuum.

### 77) PREVENT HAIRBALLS IN CATS

When a cat gags and subsequently vomits, a hairball may be the culprit. This problem occurs most frequently with long-haired cats. Felines constantly groom themselves and their buddies; some seem to be professional groomers! The process requires a feline to lick herself from nose to tail, and a great deal of her fur (especially during the hotter months) comes off during this daily chore. After it's swallowed this fur will lodge in the cat's system, until the cat expels it through the mouth. Not only are hairballs quite unappealing, but they can also irritate your cat's digestive system. Try adding a little extra virgin olive oil daily to your cat's food, and you will notice the difference. Kathy, another friend of mine and quite the cat lover, swears by this remedy for her long-haired cats.

# On the Outside . . . External

## 78) MASSAGE YOUR PET

Make your pet her very own massage oil from calendula flowers and olive oil. Calendula, a plant with brilliant yellow flowers, blooms from spring through fall. The flowers are available at health food stores all across the country. Calendula flowers are naturally antibacterial, anti-inflammatory, and antifungal. When the flowers are crushed and blended with olive oil, the resulting ointment can heal sores, cuts, eczema, psoriasis, and other difficult-to-deal-with rashes. The following healing pet massage is from Annie Bethold-Bond, at www.care2.com.

### Healing Pet Massage

- Put one handful of dried calendula flowers on the bottom of a Crock-Pot; cover completely with olive oil (1 cup)
- Place on low heat for at least 6 hours
- Cool and strain and slowly add ¼ teaspoon grapefruit seed extract
- Pour the oil into your hands and massage deeply into the coat of your pet
- This mixture will keep for 1 to 2 months if refrigerated

A note of caution: When you finish giving the massage, make sure that your pet does not roll in the dirt or jump up on your good sofa. Just as you would take a shower after your own warm-oil massage, you will need to give your pet a shower or a bath after such a treat.

The olive oil and calendula ointment may also be used to help heal dry, cracked, irritated, or itchy skin, especially bare-skin areas where a pet has scratched, chewed, or otherwise removed her fur. The ointment may also lessen scarring after wounds have healed or after stitches have been removed. If your pet licks the ointment after application, no problem. Any ingested calendula and olive oil will have additional beneficial effects on the overall healing process.

### 79) REMOVE TICKS

Now here's a trick that every pet lover will appreciate—an easy way to rid your pet of ticks. Ticks are serious pests for dogs and cats because they can transmit disease and cause discomfort and pain. If left untreated, they can cause "tick paralysis," which can lead to death. Ticks breathe oxygen, and they can be suffocated with a coat of olive oil. As the tick struggles for air, it will start to release its grasp, and may even back out on its own, without injecting its poison into your pet.

If the tick does not come out on its own, dab on more olive oil with a cotton ball to paralyze and smother it. Never squeeze the body of the tick or sharply twist it, and do not pull the tick; its head may stay imbedded. Simply apply olive oil with a cotton ball, then slowly lift the tick away from the pet's skin. Seek medical attention if you cannot remove the tick in this way.

Ear mites live inside your pet's ears, where they can cause a great deal of irritation and form a waxy material. If you notice vigorous head shaking and ear scratching, your pet may have ear mites. Any natural oil-based ear treatment (like olive oil) will ultimately drown the mites by covering their breathing pores and suffocating them. Oil can clean and heal damaged and inflamed ear canals.

The following two soothing oils can be used for your pet's ears when they're bothered by mites or after foxtails have been removed. One is made from olive oil and vitamin E; the other is made by adding mullein flowers.

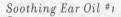

*Soothing Ear Oil #1*

- Mix 3 teaspoons of olive oil with the liquid from one 500 IU capsule of vitamin E (of course, you will need to puncture the capsule to mix)

*Soothing Ear Oil #2*

- Put about 4 ounces of mullein flowers or mullein leaves on the bottom of a Crock-Pot; cover completely with olive oil (1 cup)
- Place on low heat for at least 6 hours
- Cool and strain and pour into a glass jar

> • See the dosage instructions below
> • This mixture will keep for about one month if refrigerated

## *Dosage and Other Instructions*

First of all, wear your oldest clothing; then select a place outside or in the house where "flying" oil will not harm anything; fill your pet's ear with the soothing oil, massaging the base of the ear; wipe off the excess with a soft tissue. Repeat the process daily for three days. Then wait two days and repeat the process again. You want the ear to be clear and have no dark discharge. Check with your veterinarian if there is no improvement.

While ear infections such as those caused by ear mites often respond to olive oil herbal treatments, deeper infections (middle and inner ear) must be treated by a veterinarian. If uncertain as to what is bothering your pet's ears, make sure first to get the correct diagnosis from a veterinarian.

### 81) LUBRICATE THE SKIN ON YOUR PET'S NOSE

During the long, cold winter months, your pet's nose can become dry, cracked, and misshapen. To return this delicate area to good health, put a small amount of extra virgin olive oil on your dog's nose and very lightly massage or tap it. You may need to hold his muzzle for a few seconds after application, as dogs are great lickers. The nose will be

soothed and lubricated, and your dog will enjoy the taste of
the oil.

82) LUBRICATE YOUR DOG'S PAWS

Normal dog paws have a thick layer of tissue to protect
the delicate pads from injury and abrasion. Cracks and fis-
sures to pads are common, but they do not have to become
a big problem. During wintertime, however, paw pads (because of severe weather conditions) will often become
painfully dry and cracked. To help your dog, put a small
amount of extra virgin olive oil on his pads and gently massage it in. Just remember, distract your dog for 5 to 10 minutes so that the application will have a chance to work. If you
don't, your dog will immediately start licking it all off.

Deep cracks to a dog's pads can open up into the sensitive tissue beneath the skin. To heal this painful problem, add one teaspoon of salt to one pint of water and apply
(soak for several minutes, if you can). Then use the olive
oil massage treatment to follow up to soften the pads and
help them heal completely.

If the fur or hair between the paw pads grows too long,
it can mat and during the winter months become icy, making it very uncomfortable for your pet to walk. It's like trying to walk with a pebble in your shoe. You can trim this fur
or hair a bit for winter and then use olive oil to lubricate
this area and melt the irritating ice.

83) GIVE YOUR PET A "PETICURE"

Your dog will love you! Using warmed olive oil, massage
it into the base of the nail and onto calloused footpads to

both soften and heal. Prior to giving the peticure, lubricate the dog's nail clippers to keep them working smoothly. If you have a cat in your household, attempt a "peticure" only if you have a *very* mellow kitty.

### 84) REMOVE "ICE BALLS" FROM ANIMAL FUR

During the winter, fresh snow often attaches to the fur of animals and forms little ice balls. Fill a plastic spray bottle or a mister with olive oil and spritz it on the fur to remove the snow and ice from paws and to smooth the fur.

Now that we have reviewed the many uses of olive oil around the house and for the health and beauty of ourselves and our pets, let's turn to the centuries-old religious and ritualistic uses of this precious liquid.

# CHAPTER NINE

# Olive Oil Uses in Ritual, Religion, and Folk Magic

THROUGHOUT HISTORY, in many organized religions as well as in ancient primitive cultures, olive oil has served a variety of sacred purposes. It has been used in priestly rituals and sacred ceremonies as a symbol of purity, peace, and godliness. From the olive tree's earliest cultivation, it was thought to possess a divine nature and was revered for its hardiness and longevity as well as its fruit. The oil pressed from the fruit of the olive tree was thought to be the very essence of this divinity—a pure and shining gift received directly from the heavens. I personally feel this is still true!

The use of olive oil in sacred ritual is well known throughout the Middle East, the birthplace of several of the world's principal religions. In prebiblical religious practices and ceremonies, the oil was offered to different gods in the hope of securing special favors such as bountiful harvests, the end of neighboring rivalries, and healthy births. These and other issues were critical to early mankind. For many cultures, the fruit of the olive tree has long been a symbol of peace and reconciliation between God and mankind—ever since a dove brought an olive branch to Noah at the end of the great flood as described in the Old Testament.

In the time of the Old Testament, the Israelites burned this golden oil in the lamps that lighted their places of worship. They also used it to prepare health-giving as well as sacred ointments. So important were olives and olive oil that it is said that Moses himself exempted the men who worked in the olive groves during harvests from military duties.

In the Jewish faith, the menorah (a seven-branched candelabra) is thought to be a symbol of the nation of Israel and the mission to be "a light unto the nations" (Isaiah 42:6). A nine-branched menorah is used on Hanukkah. The tradition of celebrating Hanukkah can be attributed to a miracle involving olive oil. Hanukkah (meaning to dedicate) is celebrated each year for eight days, beginning with the twenty-fifth of Kislev (Kislev is the third month of the Jewish year). The story of Hanukkah began when the second Temple stood in Jerusalem and the Greeks ruled the Land of Israel. Eventually, the Jews rose against the persecution and religious oppression of the Greeks. When the Jews came to rededicate the Temple they wanted to light the menorah. However, they found only one small jar of ritually acceptable olive oil and lit the menorah only reluctantly, wondering if they should wait for more ritually pure olive oil to arrive. While expecting the oil to last only one day, it miraculously burned for eight days, until new ritually pure olive oil could be brought to the Temple. Since that time, the menorah is traditionally lighted for eight days during Hanukkah, as a symbol of this long-ago event. The story is celebrated in the old city of Modiin in Israel, where a huge olive press re-creates the Hanukkah legend and the Feast of Oil.

Some local Jewish communities feature olive oil pressing as Hanukkah approaches, and children learn the historical significance of olives and olive oil. The tradition is further reinforced at Kehillah Jewish High School in San Jose, California, where each student, in his or her first year, is given a small olive oil–burning Hanukkah lamp. The lamp symbolizes that they can accomplish miracles in their lives and overcome obstacles.

Children at Jewish schools are further introduced to the importance of the olive tree during Tu B'Shvat, a holiday when thanks are given for different species of growing things, including the olive tree. The song "Atzay Zaytim Omdim" ("The Olive Tree Is Standing") is a traditional song that virtually all Jewish children sing.

An eternal light (*Ner Tamid*), which hangs above the ark in every synagogue, is never extinguished. Symbolizing God's eternal presence, the *Ner Tamid* was traditionally a lamp filled with olive oil. Today, most are fueled by either gas or electric lightbulbs.

In Islam, olive oil is described as a symbol for the light that shines without being touched by fire: "Allah is the light of the heavens and earth. . . . Within the lamp a brilliant star lit by a blessed tree, an olive tree, neither of the East nor of the West, the oil of which could shine without being touched by fire; Light upon Light" (Koran 24:35).

In Christianity, much is written in the New Testament Gospels about the sanctification (purification, or making "holy") of olive oil and the sacredness of the olive tree. For instance, the Garden of Gethsemane, well known as the place where Christ is said to have prayed on the night he was to be arrested, was actually located on the Mount of Olives. The word *Gethsemane* comes from the words *geth* (press, wine press) and *semane* or *shemen* (oil/olive oil), so the word Gethsemane itself can be translated to mean "the press for olive oil." In the Christian faith, this precious pressed oil was used to generate light and for anointing.

## 85) ANOINT DURING BAPTISM AND CONFIRMATION

All the Christian faiths that have retained sacramental rites use olive oil in their sacred rituals and ceremonies. In many Christian churches, there are separate categories of sacred olive oil that are used in the ceremonies involving anointing. For example, there are blessed olive oils called Oil of the Sick (used to anoint the sick and dying), the Oil of Catechumens (used to anoint one into the faith during baptism), and Chrism Oil or Myron Oil (consecrated olive oil infused with perfumed balm or perfumed oil also used to baptize and confirm people into the faith, to ordain priests, and to consecrate churches and chalices). There is a symbolic reason for the addition of a perfumed balm or balsam to some of the consecrated olive oil. Olive oil represents the outpouring of sacramental grace, and balsam, which is quite fragrant, signifies the sweetness of Christian virtue.

These sacred oils are blessed once a year at a centrally located church or cathedral (for example, by a bishop in the

Roman Catholic Church or by a bishop in the Greek Orthodox Church) and distributed to their respective churches.

The use of olive oil in religious ritual dates back at least
to the Greeks. We know this fact because the word *chrism*
comes from the Greek word *chrisma*, which means anointing. This particular sacred oil is extra virgin olive oil mixed
with a scented balsam. When the oil is used in an anointing
ceremony or ritual, the priest usually applies it in a cross
formation. This is to remind Christians that all blessings
come from the crucified Christ, who in their belief system
is the source of all healing and life for the world.

## Baptism

In the ceremony of baptism, an individual is made a
servant of God and thus a true member of his faith. As the
child (or adult) is anointed with the special oil (for example, chrism oil), he is deemed to be endowed with the Holy
Spirit for Christian life and mission. Metaphorically, this
anointing recalls the descent of the Holy Spirit on Jesus at
his baptism in the Jordan River, according to Mark 1:9–11.
In turn, this recalls the words of the "Servant of the Lord"
in the book of Isaiah, 61:1–3: "The spirit of the Lord God is
upon me, because the Lord has anointed me; he has sent
me to bring good news to the oppressed. . . ."

Baptisms are solemn yet festive events, similar to
weddings. The planning of a formal baptism includes a
great many details, including making the many church
and post-ceremony arrangements. Prior to the baptism,

the parents select a couple to stand in as godparents for the child being baptized. An adult going through a baptism ceremony is free to select his or her own godparents. Both the parents and godparents then attend instructional classes, which include a thorough explanation of the ceremony and the meanings of the water and olive oil.

The actual amount of olive oil used during this ceremony varies within different Christian churches. In the Greek Orthodox Church, a child or adult is completely covered with olive oil (if you've seen *My Big Fat Greek Wedding*, you will have an idea of this part of the ceremony); in the Roman Catholic Church, a simple anointing of the forehead is performed.

While baptisms are indeed serious events, I'd like to share a humorous story that happened to a friend of mine at a recent baptism. As is the custom so often today, the baptismal ceremony was to be videotaped. The godparents of the new baby asked my friend Brent to videotape the child's baptism at a Greek Orthodox Church. Brent felt confident of his ability as a videographer to handle this task. When he first arrived, he watched the priest bless the water in the baptismal font and then saw him add a small amount of the olive oil (that had been brought to the church by the godparents, as is custom). Brent thought this was pretty much all there was to a baptism!

But then . . . things got interesting. During the next part of the ceremony, the godparents proceeded to undress plump little Nicholas. This undressing symbolically represents the removal of old sin. The priest proceeded to make the sign of the cross with oil on various parts of the infant. Then the godparents carefully began to rub olive oil all over

Nicholas's body. At this time, Brent's real video challenge began! A *very* slick Nicholas began to slip and slide and almost slithered through the hands of the godparents; at any moment Brent expected to see the poor little guy dropped on his head. Consequently, Brent was moving the camera all over the place, trying to capture every part of the baptism. The video portrays an otherwise solemn ceremony in quite a humorous manner!

When the godparents finally handed the baby to the priest, Brent breathed a huge sigh of relief and recorded the remainder of the ceremony with a steady hand. To complete Nicholas's baptism, the priest immersed the baby three times into the baptismal font (symbolizing the three days that Christ spent in the tomb). At the end of the ceremony, the godparents happily dressed the baby in new white clothing to absorb the remaining holy oil. At the end of the ceremony everyone was thankful that the baby had not slipped through the godparents' hands, and Brent went on to the post-baptism party, where he drank more than a few glasses of ouzo in celebration!

## Chrismation and Confirmation

Little Nicholas also received a second sacrament during his baptism (called Chrismation); this sacrament corresponds to Confirmation (received when a child is about thirteen years old) in the Roman Catholic Church. This sacrament represents the gift of God's grace, which will help the child to lead a strong Christian life. Again, olive oil is the base oil of anointment.

## 86) ANOINT THE SICK AND DYING

Often referred to as the sacrament Unction, in Extreme Unction or, more recently, Sacrament of Anointing the Sick, the sick and dying of many Christian faiths are anointed with the blessed olive oil. The sick are anointed, as the need arises, on the affected part of their bodies. In the Letter of James 5:14, found in the New Testament, a passage reads as follows: "Is any among you sick? Let him call for the elders of the church, and let them pray over him, anointing him with oil in the name of the Lord, and the Lord will raise him up." In Isaiah 61:3, in the Old Testament, there is a passage that metaphorically speaks of the oil given for joy instead of mourning.

In the Church of Jesus Christ of Latter-Day Saints (Mormon Church), tiny vials of consecrated olive oil are carried by Elders and applied to people who are sick or afflicted, thereby needing a blessing from God. Many families keep small bottles of consecrated olive oil in their medicine cabinets for use by a Priesthood bearer in blessing family members who are ill.

## 87) ANOINT DURING THE ORDINATION OF PRIESTS

The special infused (chrism) olive oil is also used to anoint priests at their ordination. During this most sacred of holy rituals, a new priest's hands are often anointed with the sign of the cross. An older tradition was for chrism oil to be placed on the palms of the priests; then their hands were bound in linen wrappings, thus securing the oil and their faith. The parents of the priest would then remove the cloth bindings. Parents and relatives vied for the honor of embroidering the cloth, which was thereafter kept in the family as a precious souvenir.

## 88) CONSECRATE ALTARS, CHURCHES, CHALICES, AND BELLS

To "consecrate" means to make holy or set apart for God's purposes. Once again, olive oil is the base oil used in the consecration of altars and church buildings (Exodus 29:7, Luke 4:18). In addition, this chrism oil is also used to consecrate chalices and patens (the plates for holding the bread in a Eucharistic service) and to bless new bells prior to their being placed in church bell towers.

## 89) BURN IT IN ALTAR LAMPS

For centuries, olive oil has been used for illumination in shrines and chapels and for burning in altar lamps in churches and cathedrals. In the Old Testament (Exodus 27: 20–21) it is written that God commanded "a lamp filled with the purest oil of olives should always burn before the curtain that veiled the Holy of Holies." The Roman Catholic Church, as prescribed by ritual (Rituale Romanum iv: 6) states that at least "one lamp, preferably fueled by olive oil or bee's wax, is to be kept burning before the tabernacle" (a tabernacle is the small enclosure for consecrated breads). This lamp is not an ornament for the altar, but is intended to remind parishioners of the presence of Christ through light.

As many look to this burning lamp as a symbol and as a reminder to profess their love for God, it also has more practical references, as evidenced in the New Testament

(Matthew 25), which describes the parable of the wise and foolish bridesmaids and the marriage custom of meeting the bridegroom with burning oil lamps to light the way and escort him into the house. It also gives us a glimpse into the cultural importance of this precious ooze of the olive and how important it was (and is) to keep olive oil on hand for illumination when "the foolish bridesmaids did not have enough oil to keep their lamps burning, they had to go off to buy some, and were too late for the wedding feast."

### 90) FOSTER SUPERSTITIONS

There are also ancient superstitions connected with olive oil. Some believe that, during baptism in the Greek Orthodox Church, an unoiled part of a baby's body will either smell for the rest of the child's life or be weak. This superstition is somewhat reminiscent of the fabled washing of Achilles. His mother held him by the heel during his baptism (in water), and his heel turned out to be the weakest part of his body.

On a recent trip to Tuscany, I went to several olive farms that had producing olive oil mills to witness the November harvesting of olives and the pressing of the oil. My cousin Karry and I joined eighteen other olive oil aficionados on an eight-day, fun-filled, sumptuously delicious, educationally rich tour. We were able to pick olives, then watch the transporting and washing, and the pressing and the separation process. At one of the mills, our guide placed a pitcher under a spout and we watched the new, green aromatic olive oil pour out. We were each given a slice of toast and dutifully stood in line as the guide poured the new oil on the bread. A lot of drizzling and a lot of oohs and aahs. The proprietor of this farm told me of an old olive oil superstition. She explained, "If someone has an eye infection, all one needs to do is look inside a bottle of olive oil and the infection will disappear." I wish my dear father, who was an eye doctor, were still alive. I would ask him and other optometrists and ophthalmologists everywhere to try this with their patients and let me know the results of their "research."

### 91) USE IN MAGICAL POTIONS

A friend, Elisabetta, from Siena told me that olive oil is still thought of as a magical potion that offers the hope of various positive outcomes, not the least of which is thought to be the power to drive away misfortune: "I know it was quite common for my grandmothers in Tuscany and Umbria to use olive oil to send away bad luck or evil power caused by other people. They used to fill a soup plate with water and pour some olive oil on top of it: if the oil spreads in big spots, it means that someone is sending some evil and, to get it resolved, you have to repeat this operation regularly until the spots become smaller."

There are many other magical folk beliefs associated with olive trees and olive oil. It has most historically been used in rituals of protection, healing, or peace. Still today, people often hang an olive branch over a front door in order to guard against all manner of evils; they put an olive branch on the chimney to prevent lightning; they set small olive leaf crosses in the fields to protect the harvests; and, to cure a headache, they write Athena's name on an olive leaf and press it against their head! Some people scatter olive leaves in a room to foster peaceful vibration or wear them on the body for luck. Throughout history, olive oil has represented an emotional, spiritual, sensual, and culinary journey—no wonder this very special oil has maintained its magic for so long and with so many diverse cultures.

In the following chapter, you are invited to taste the oil and use its magical qualities on any number of special occasions. As we learned in the parable of the wise and foolish bridesmaids, one should never "foolishly" run out of olive oil prior to a special celebration or party. I was raised by my family always to be prepared—particularly for special occasions. In my next chapter, I am going to relate some ways to host truly unique parties and use olive oil for special occasions.

# CHAPTER TEN

# Parties and Special Occasions with Olive Oil

I RECENTLY READ an article in the *San Francisco Chronicle* that said a "Los Gatos couple won't leave home without their olive oil" and that "wherever they go out to eat . . . [they] . . . take along a bottle of their own olive oil." They, quite literally, take their own estate-bottled olive oil, as they are the owners of Olivas de Oro, an olive company in northern California. Maybe this news article is a precursor of days to come, when customers will request by name the brand and type of olive oil they want to consume with their meal at a restaurant. Just as we used to order either a simple red or white wine, today's sophisticated diners now request specific varietals or blends of wine—for example, a "spicy Merlot" or "big Cabernet," a "buttery Chardonnay" or a "light Pinot Grigio." People often ask for a wine blended by a specific vineyard: "I will have the Santa Margherita Pinot Grigio." Can similar requests for specific cultivars and producers of extra virgin olive oil be in the not-so-distant future? My feeling is that this time will come very soon.

Olive oil is following exactly the same sophisticated path as wines in other ways as well. Labels on some olive oils designate not only the country from which they come (that is the law) but also the specific region or state (for example, Tuscany, Liguria, Puglia, Provence, or California). Some olive oils are also labeled with the specific type of cultivar, meaning type of olive (for example, Arbequina, Frantoio, or Mission). Still others are described as a Bold Picual or a Sweet Hojiblanca. Each year, at the Sonoma Olive Festival Founder's Dinner, olive oils are paired with courses, which are paired with wines, during a wonderfully sumptuous seven-course dinner. Other festivals and restaurants are doing the same.

So how do you decide which of the many olive oils you prefer? The only way to find your favorite olive oil is to taste as many of them as you can. You can do this by yourself, with your family and friends, or at an organized "olive oil–tasting event." Olive oil tastings are becoming popular in cutting-edge restaurants, well-stocked kitchen and gourmet gift stores, and in homes across the United States. These special tastings can be great fun and provide for excellent social interaction as well as help you and your friends appreciate and learn about the many qualities and tastes of extra virgin olive oil.

In California, where 99 percent of the olives in the United States are grown, olive oil tastings are very popular. Olives have been part of California's rich agricultural heritage since Spanish missionaries brought in the first olive trees. Many of these olive groves, which are being restored through MOPREP (Mission Olive Preservation and Education Project), can still be seen today at the California mission sites, including Mission San Francisco Solano de Sonoma.

Each year in Sonoma, the "Season of the Olive" is celebrated with an annual Olive Festival. The festival transforms the winter months from December through February into "a celebration of the senses" as people are invited to "see, sip, savor, and celebrate the season of the olive." The festival begins with a Blessing of the Olives ceremony. At last year's festival, Father Aurelio Villa referenced both a household and a spiritual use of olive oil in his blessing, as he eloquently commented, "Do you know that olive oil can even take the rust out of metal? Yet, the most rusted part may be in our hearts, so let's put a drop of olive oil in our hearts and live and shine in peace and love." A truly memorable comment befitting the opening ceremony. For three months, events and activities filled with food, art, music, and a few martinis make this festival a must when you visit this lovely area of northern California.

In addition to this event, each year from October through December, olive-picking opportunities abound when many producers will actually invite people who have an interest in olives and olive oil to come and help handpick the olives (or see the olives harvested in other ways). During this time, the rancher traditionally offers the helpers a lunch and a trip to the olive mill or *frantoio* (meaning olive oil processing mill in Italian, and it's the name of a specific cultivar or type of olive). Frantoio is also the name of a great restaurant in Mill Valley, California, the only restaurant in the United States where you can watch olives being pressed (during the season), while eating a delicious meal.

Outside of California, in olive-producing countries, especially in the Mediterranean area, similar harvest events are held. The Internet is a great source of information for locating these events, and I would suggest checking the list in the back of this book if you are planning a trip to California, Italy, Greece, France, or Spain during the months of October, November, or December. You may also wish to attend the Sensory Evaluation of Olive Oil course held annually at the University of California at Davis, as part of UCD extension offerings (www.extension.ucdavis.edu) or you may wish to contact the ONAOO (Organizzazione Nazionale Assaggiatori Olio di Oliva—the National Organization for the Tasting of Olive Oil) at www.oliveoil.org and take a course while visiting the Italian Riviera. Not only will you learn a great deal more about the process of making olive oil and the taste of the liquid gold, you will be able to add a completely new skill set to your "résumé"!

As I mentioned, olive oil tastings are popular events, not only in California but throughout the United States (and around the world) in many well-known specialty retail stores such as Williams-Sonoma and Oliviers & Co. They are also popular in gourmet markets, such as Whole Foods, Dean & DeLuca, Corti Brothers (in Sacramento), Zabar's (in New York) and Zingerman's (in Ann Arbor).

People come from all over the world to be educated and meet renowned olive oil expert Darrell Corti of Corti Brothers store. He often consults and lectures worldwide on all aspects of olive oil, and his newsletters are filled with products and information to "enliven, excite, improve and otherwise make delicious" your food experiences. Another well-known store (with a delightful, witty mail-order catalog), Zingerman's, offers a wide selection of olive oils and provides specialized training in customer service, merchandising, and specialty foods for retailers. A friend of mine attended one of their training seminars. On the very first day, the participants were asked: "Who came the farthest distance?" She won (having traveled from Nevada to Michigan) and was awarded a gift called "Travel Oil"—a hip flask–sized bottle of olive oil—just like the one I have always included in my trusty carry-on bag! When my friend returned to her seat, another member of the seminar inquired of the moderator, "Why olive oil?" She responded that a traveler could use the Travel Oil in so many ways, including using the oil to make a small meal by "buying some bread and dipping away." So remember this tip if you find yourself stranded at an airport by those inevitable flight delays—you'll never go hungry traveling with your flask of olive oil.

Olive oil can be used as a hostess gift for parties and events and can make lovely gifts for special occasions. Your hostess will be most appreciative of your gift, as it will serve so many purposes. Every day, more and more people are discovering that they actually need to have on hand several olive oils to suit their cooking needs (and other needs). Just as people prefer different wines with different cuisines, people also prefer different olive oils to add distinct flavors. So, next time you think to bring flowers or wine to your hosts, think again and gift them with the treat of a special bottle of extra virgin olive oil.

*Parties*

## 92) ORGANIZE AN OLIVE OIL–TASTING PARTY

An olive oil–tasting party is a unique way of helping both you and your friends develop your individual tastes for good olive oil. Just as wine-tasting events have become popular gourmet experiences, you can now dazzle your friends with your newly found knowledge of olive oil while at the same time introducing them to the many healthful and gastronomical qualities of extra virgin olive oil.

Traditionally, olive oil has been tasted and judged using several methods, for instance—on bread, on boiled rice, from a glass, or from a teaspoon. Olive oil is valued for its culinary attributes and also for its organoleptic properties: flavor (*sapore*), bouquet (*aroma*), and color (*colore*). It triggers sensations in four out of our five senses, whether olfactory (smell), gustative (taste), tactile (touch), or visual (sight). The time of harvest, oil-extraction method, variety of tree, climate, and soil can add to your organoleptic assessment of different oils, just as these same factors affect the taste of wines.

To help you with your olive oil tasting parties, see the Olive Oil Tasting Score Sheet for Drizzle It On . . . Parties on page 175. To conduct an olive oil tasting in your home, assemble four or five different extra virgin olive oils. You may choose oils from the same state or regions (for example: California or Tuscany); you may choose from different regions within the same country (for example: Tuscany, Liguria, and Calabria), or from different countries (for example: France, Italy, Spain, Greece, United States), or from different cultivars (for example: Arbequina, Frantoio, Koroneiki, or Nocellàra). You will also need small tasting glasses (small plastic glass will do), sliced apples (for refreshing the mouth after tasting), and paper cups (for the expectoration of the olive oil after each tasting).

During any tasting, you will taste for defects as well as for positive attributes. The reason you check first for defects is that extra virgin olive oil must be free of defects. Defects include any flavor(s) that can be described as fusty, musty, winey-vinegary, muddy sediment, metallic, or rancid. If there are no defects, then positive attributes are judged. Positive attributes include any flavor(s) that can be described as olive fruity, pleasantly bitter, or pungent.

## Olive Oil–Tasting Party

- First cleanse the palate by eating a slice of apple
- Pour about 1 tablespoon of extra virgin olive oil into a small glass
- Cup the glass in your palm to warm it (to room temperature) and cover the top with your other hand (to keep the scent from volatizing)
- Hold the glass tightly and swirl the oil for a minute
- Uncover the top and bring the glass to your nose and inhale slowly several times
- Sip a small amount, about 1½ teaspoons, and roll it lightly in your mouth as you would a wine. (Judge the "mouthfeel"; is it smooth and light or greasy?)
- Suck in air through your teeth to discover the flavors. (An unavoidable sound will be heard.) Keep the oil in your mouth for at least 10 seconds
- Spit the olive oil into a paper cup. (If you swallow the olive oil, no problem.)
- Decide if you like it or not! Or use a score sheet and record your responses (you will need a separate score sheet for each oil tasted)
- Discuss your assessment with others
- Cleanse the palate with a fresh apple slice before proceeding to the next oil

NOTE: For your tasting party, you can use small plastic glasses (one for each olive oil tasted)

## Olive Oil Tasting—What to Look For . . .

### SIGHT

- While professional tasters use blue glasses so as not to be influenced by the color of the olive oil, you can study its color. Color ranges from light yellow to an intense green.

### SMELL

- Take a good sniff to assess the fresh and fruity aroma (of a good oil)

### TASTE

- Since tasting olive oil is a new experience for most of us, it is difficult to find the words to describe the different flavors.
- Some familiar terms are often used to help describe the flavor of positive attributes—for example, the flavors of apple, grass, almond, and artichoke
- Positive attributes include:

  Fresh olive fruitiness—is it ripe or more green?

  Bitterness—as it moves through the palate; is it a pleasant bitter taste?

  Pungency—is there a biting sensation in the whole mouth and later in the throat?

- Defects are easier to detect and are defined by the following descriptive terms:

  Fusty—from olives stored in piles that have undergone fermentation

  Musty—from yeasts or fungus in olives stored in humid conditions

  Muddy sediment—from prolonged contact with sediment in storage containers

  Winey-vinegary—due to the fermentation of the olives

  Metallic—from contact with metals during processing

  Rancid—from oxidation (the worst defect and the easiest to detect)

When tasting several oils, start off with the oil with the mildest flavor (for example, a late-harvest oil); save your early-harvest or green oil for one of the last. Also, taste lower-quality oil last, as defects can seriously affect tasting and can lead to an incorrect sensory analysis of better-quality oils. One additional tip for the party: if you can smell a major defect in the oil, there is no need to taste it; your olfactory analysis will be enough. And now, some additional tasting rules . . . which are hard to enforce at a party!

### Hard-to-Enforce Olive Oil—Tasting Rules

- Don't taste if you have a cold
- Do not use perfumes or scented deodorants
- No tasting after tobacco, coffee, or a heavy meal
- Best time to taste is in the morning after breakfast (wait at least 1 hour)—taste and olfactory perception is highest in the morning hours

Here is a score sheet you can use for what I call . . . "drizzle it on" parties.

## OLIVE OIL TASTING SCORE SHEET

*For Drizzle It On . . . Parties*

Name_____ Sample Oil _____ Rating_____

**WHAT TO LOOK FOR:**
- *Sight*
  Study the color of the oil. Color ranges from light yellow to an
  intense green color.
- *Smell*
  Take a good sniff to assess the fresh and fruity aroma.
- *Taste*
  First look for the defects, then assess the positive attributes.

**PERCEPTION OF DEFECTS:**
- *Rancid*:          0 _____ 5 _____ 10
  (The taste of old olive oil)
- *Others* (specify):   0 _____ 5 _____ 10
  (Fusty, musty, muddy sediment, winey-vinegary, metallic)

0 = None |  1–4 = Slight |  5–6 = Average |  above 6 = Great to Extreme
If Rancid—use around the house, not in and on your body!

**PERCEPTION OF POSITIVE ATTRIBUTES:**
- *Fruity*:          0 _____ 5 _____ 10
  (Fresh olive fruitiness)
- *Bitter*:          0 _____ 5 _____ 10
  (As it moves through the palate, is it a pleasant bitter taste?)
- *Pungent*:          0 _____ 5 _____ 10
  (A biting sensation in the whole mouth and later in the throat)

0–2.5 = Low Intensity |  2.5–5.5 = Medium Intensity |  above 5.5 = High Intensity

In addition to straight olive oil tasting, there are other ways to taste different olive oils. Dip a piece of bread in the olive oil. Take care to rinse your mouth with water or wine between tastings. Another way is to steam and slice a potato and dip the potato slice in olive oil. Refresh your mouth afterward by eating a piece of apple.

And, naturally, you may wish to taste the oils with different combinations of foods. Each guest could bring a bottle of his or her favorite olive oil accompanied by an appetizer made with that same oil. You really don't need much preparation for this party—just two or three different oils, a few simple dishes, and those friends who have a keen interest in the gourmet world. Forget the rules and the score sheets, and just enjoy a really good time!

### 93) HOST A *"PROVA DEL PANE"* PARTY

Another way to test and taste olive oil is with *la prova del pane* (the bread test) or the ritual of the *fett'unta* (oiled slice), a simple ceremony that celebrates the new olive oil harvest each year. In Tuscany, usually in early November, the neighbors and friends of a community will gather together with their new, freshly pressed oil. They'll grill sliced bread over a fire, rub the bread with a clove of garlic, and then proudly drizzle the bread with the new oil. You may think that this "recipe" sounds like a lot like a basic bruschetta, and you are right. *Fett'unta* and bruschetta are two words for the same dish, although bruschetta is more widely adopted. The difference is that *fett'unta* (well known in Florence) puts the emphasis on tasting the olive oil itself, while bruschetta (well known in other parts of central Italy) is intended to emphasize the charring or burning of the bread. Bruschetta typically adds another topping to the olive oil and bread.

You could (well, almost) replicate this annual *fett'unta* ritual, and you can easily replicate the many types of bruschetta. All you need for the ritual is an open fireplace (so that the bread can be grilled on both sides over the embers of a fire), day-old country-style bread, cloves of garlic, salt, and an abundant amount of the best extra virgin olive oil available. Of course, if you don't have the open fire, you can grill the bread by broiling it in the oven.

Here are a couple of recipes that could be served at your *Prova del Pane* party. Make sure that you "wash" these delicious treats down with a glass or two of Chianti Classico or your favorite Sangiovese.

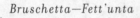

### Bruschetta—Fett'unta

Slices of country-style bread
Several cloves of fresh garlic
Extra virgin olive oil
Salt

HOW TO PREPARE

- Grill the bread (on both sides)
- Rub the bread, while it is still warm, with a clove of garlic
- Pour extra virgin olive oil on each slice of bread
- Sprinkle with salt

### Bruschetta al Pomodoro—Tomato Bruschetta

1 pound ripe tomatoes
2 cloves fresh garlic,
   finely chopped
1 handful fresh basil,
   finely chopped
1 tablespoon oregano

Pinch of peperoncino
Salt and pepper
1 cup extra virgin olive oil
6 slices country-style
   bread

**HOW TO PREPARE**

- Immerse the tomatoes in very hot water, then in cold water, and peel
- Chop tomatoes into small pieces and add garlic, basil, peperoncino, and salt and pepper
- Add extra virgin olive oil and marinate at room temperature for at least 1 hour
- Just before serving, grill the bread
- Place each slice on a plate and top with the sauce or put the sauce in a bowl and let your guests spoon their own sauce onto their bread

Before we leave this party, just note that raw (yes, raw!) artichokes are also perfect with the new oil. They both have the same sort of bite! Put extra virgin olive oil over paper-thin slices of young, raw artichoke hearts, add a bit of shaved parmesan cheese and a pinch of salt, and you have *carpaccio di carciofi.* Try it.

*Special Occasions*

### 94) PREPARE FAVORS FOR WEDDINGS

How would you like your guests to remember your special day? Look no further for that unique and interesting favor for your wedding. You can arrange to have a "privately labeled" small bottle of extra virgin olive oil made for each guest, or you can make your own favors, using small bottles and filling them with extra virgin olive oil. I have attended several weddings of late where bottles of olive oil were the favors. They were a great hit, and you can well imagine the many clever comments made at the dinner tables about how the guests were going to use the oil after the reception. Next time I will have to listen more closely for any comments I may want to include in my next book!

### 95) GO TO AN OLIVE OIL—WRESTLING COMPETITION

The village of Kirkpinar, Turkey, has been holding an annual oil-wrestling festival for centuries. It is a tradition that has lasted for over six hundred years and dates back to the Turks' exodus from central Asia. It is a simple athletic competition in which big, burly men wearing leather pants pour olive oil over their bare chests and then, with oil glistening over their rippling muscles, wrestle. The goal is to pin the other wrestler to the ground, and the competition culminates with the winner being awarded the Golden Belt.

As I understand it, there is quite an "unsportsmanlike" tactic to this event. A common practice is to stick a hand down an opponent's leather pants. I guess one can get a better grip! (Oops . . . does this use of olive oil belong in another chapter?)

### 96) CREATE OLIVE GIFT BASKETS

Gift baskets are always popular for holidays, birthdays, and any special occasion. You can create your own olive gift basket and fill it with various olive oils, an assortment of jars of yummy tapenades, several varieties of cured olives, and other tasty delicacies. Also, you may wish to include olive-themed ceramics (like olive boats or olive serving bowls and dishes), olive oil books (including this one!), olive-printed table linens, olive-themed paper napkins, and olive oil containers. You probably have your own local gourmet retail specialty store that sells some of these items, or you can find great websites featuring olive oil and unique gift baskets.

Another idea is to give just a hand-printed "massage certificate" in a gift basket and include a bottle of extra virgin olive oil and this book, for a few additional ideas. A massage is a most wonderful personal gift since your time and energy are focused on pleasing and relaxing that special someone. (Oops . . . does this use also belong in another chapter?)

### 97) BUY OR MAKE FLAVORED OLIVE OILS

Of late, we see a newer category of olive oils offered for sale—the flavored or infused olive oils. It is true that olive oil flavors blend well with lemons and oranges, and with many herbs, including basil, fennel, sage, rosemary, thyme, and tarragon. There are many excellent flavored olive oils on the shelves in markets. However, with the availability of superb extra virgin olive oils and the year-round availability of lemons and herbs (fresh and dried), making your own infusions as you need them is easy. If you wish to make your own garlic oil, I find it is best to use dried or roasted garlic; fresh garlic tends to spoil.

If you do decide to make infused oil, it is important that you use very clean bottles and that you store the herb-filled bottles properly (in the refrigerator). Use the oil within three weeks. If the bottles are not stored properly, the oil will become rancid and may be dangerous to your health. This guarded comment is relevant only if you make infused oils. Store-purchased infused oils are safe and will indicate their freshness and appropriate use on the label.

### One Way of Making Flavored Olive Oil

½ cup chopped fresh herbs
   or several dry sprigs or
   leaves—to taste (e.g.,
   rosemary, sage, thyme)
1 cup extra virgin olive oil

HOW TO PREPARE

- Place ingredients in a nonmetal pan
- Gently sauté the herbs in the oil until fragrant (about 5 minutes)
- Do not let this mixture come to a boil
- Strain, place in bottles, and store in the refrigerator

I have included several additional recipes for infused oils in the next chapter. There are also several books on the market that are devoted solely to the making of flavored or infused oils. See the Bibliography for a few additional ideas.

### 98) JOIN AN OLIVE OIL CLUB

What better way to learn more about your newly discovered passion (you are passionate by now, right?!) than to join an olive oil club. I belong to several olive oil clubs and organizations. Each offers valuable information on our favorite subject. Whether it's meeting interesting people, being introduced to new olive oils, getting to buy great products, or joining in on educational and fun events, being a member of an olive oil club will make you the envy of all your friends. I've listed several stores and websites in the references section that offer these opportunities.

### 99) LEARN OLIVE OIL TRIVIA TO AMAZE YOUR FAMILY AND FRIENDS

Just think, in case you are ever a contestant on *Jeopardy*, *Who Wants to Be a Millionaire*, or *Hollywood Squares* and are asked a question about the olive and its oil, you will know the answer if you learn olive oil trivia. And what better way than to review this book or to read the books that appear in the Bibliography. Who knows, someday a whole section of Cranium or Trivial Pursuit may be devoted to olives and olive oil, and you will delight your family and friends with your knowledge.

## 100) BYOOO (BRING YOUR OWN OLIVE OIL)— BECAUSE EVERY OCCASION IS SPECIAL

We have all seen casual invitations to parties where BYOB (Bring Your Own Booze) was scribbled at the bottom of the paper. Just as my friend won the Travel Oil from Zingerman's and the couple from Los Gatos brought their own olive oil to the restaurant, we may just see a new acronym arise—BYOOO (Bring Your Own Olive Oil). I always keep several small bottles of extra virgin olive oil on hand in a dark cupboard. When visiting a friend or going to a dinner party, I give olive oil. I suggest you do the same.

Since you never know when you will be invited to an impromptu party or when an occasion may call for a special gift, you will be prepared—armed with your very own bottle of extra virgin olive oil.

# CHAPTER ELEVEN

# Cooking Ideas

FINALLY, after learning of so many different ways you can effectively use olive oil, we arrive at use #101, and it is the one most of us associate with the golden oil—cooking. With its unique flavor and delicious aroma (especially when sautéed with onions and garlic), olive oil is finally becoming a *must-have* staple in American kitchens across the country, achieving the culinary importance that other parts of the world have given it for thousands of years.

There are many excellent cookbooks on the market whose main focus is olive oil; several are listed in the Bibliography. Many of these books describe how olive oil is an integral ingredient in various types of Mediterranean cooking, and how it forms the basis of this region's well-known recipes. In fact, my Genovese background attests to the fact that, as stated in *Enchanted Liguria,* "*The single ingredient in almost every Ligurian recipe is olive oil.*"

In fact, I love talking to people about how they use

olive oil in cooking and what oils they use for which cooking purpose. One of my best friends, Angela, is from the city of Bologna. She is one of the best chefs I know. When I asked her about her early recollections of olive oil, she told me that when she was a very small child, her *nonna* would ask her what she wanted for a snack: *pane con chocolate* (bread and Nutella—a chocolate spread), *pane con marmalatta* (bread and jam), or *pane con olio de oliva* (bread and olive oil). She always answered *pane con olio de oliva* and to this day would choose bread drizzled with olive oil over the other choices. She lovingly refers to olive oil as "a taste of heaven."

Olive oil's versatility offers great variety in cooking situations. I use extra virgin olive oils for my cooking needs and keep several types readily available, proudly displayed on my kitchen counter. I use special estate-bottled extra virgin olive oils to drizzle over fish, salads, and vegetables; and quality extra virgin olive oils for cooking and for most of the other uses mentioned in this book. I have included a chart for suggested uses for different cooking functions at the end of the book, under Olive Oil Usage Guidelines.

However, to many, the decision of which olive oil to use depends upon personal taste. A light, fruity olive oil (in terms of both color and taste) can be used in dishes when you do not want a dominant olive oil taste. I am *not* referring to the labeling "extra light," which is a refined olive oil that has light or nonexistent taste. I am referring here to late-harvest extra virgin olive oil, which often exhibits more subtle and delicate flavors. However, remember "light" never means "fewer calories"; as I have stated before: All olive oil has the same number of calories—120 calories per tablespoon.

What follows are a few cooking tips (and recipes) from my family, friends, and noted chef Erik Cosselmon of Cetrella Bistro and Café in Half Moon Bay, California. From appetizers to main dishes, olive oil enhances any meal.

*Drizzle It On . . .*

### DRIZZLE IT ON . . . USING OLIVE OIL IN ITS RAW STATE

Undoubtedly the best way to savor the special taste is to use extra virgin olive oil "raw," that is, straight from the bottle at room temperature. In its raw state, your senses will come alive when you experience its unadulterated flavor, whether it is drizzled on a plate of freshly sliced tomatoes or drizzled on that steak, hot off the grill. The aroma, the bouquet, the taste—to say nothing of the "mouthfeel"—all will be heightened with that final drizzle. Olive oil adds body to food and serves to balance the acidity in certain dishes.

Because olive oil is so flavorful, only a small amount is necessary to bring out the peak flavor in a great many foods. Of course, in these examples, your best extra virgin olive oil is a must!

---

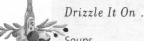

*Drizzle It On . . .*

Soups

Fish

Steak

Sliced tomatoes and other vegetables

Baked potatoes

Popcorn

Pizza dough

And, of course . . . bread and salads

Speaking of salads, good-quality extra virgin olive oil is crucial in the preparation of great salad dressings. In a dressing, you can realize the full flavor of olive oil. Different types of olive oils will give different results, so I recommend that you experiment with different olive oils to determine your personal favorite. For salads, I prefer to drizzle the olive oil on first, coating the lettuce and other fresh ingredients and then adding the vinegar or lemon and salt to taste. However, some people prefer to add the acidic ingredients (vinegar, lemon juice, etc.) to the salad first and then add the olive oil. This reversal of order gives an entirely different taste to the salad dressing.

One of my favorite, unique vegetable dishes courtesy of Erik, utilizes the "drizzle it on . . ." technique. When combined with pecorino cheese, the dressing becomes creamy and delicious.

*Fava Beans with Pecorino*   (SERVES 6)

2 cups peeled fava beans
1 cup crumbled fresh
   pecorino cheese
Small pinch of salt

1 teaspoon cracked black
   pepper
½ cup extra virgin olive oil

- Mix the favas with the cheese, salt, and pepper
- Drizzle with olive oil and toss until creamy
- Serve at room temperature

## USE INFUSED OR FLAVORED OILS . . . FOR DIPPING OR DRIZZLING

The variety of infused or flavored oils is endless. Here are some rules that Erik follows when making infused oils: (1) If the herbs are bruised or discolored, they should be blanched (scalded in hot water) and shocked (put in cold water) and wrung out; (2) Dried herbs, like thyme and rosemary, work better when the oil is warmed; and (3) Oils made from citrus work best if the fruit is zested (use a zester to capture very thin pieces of orange peel or lemon peel) over a bowl of the olive oil to catch all the volatile oil properties. And remember, use very clean bottles and store the infused oils properly in the refrigerator for no more than three weeks.

### Chive Oil

1 bunch chives cut into
  1-inch pieces
1 cup extra virgin olive oil (at
  room temperature)
Small pinch of salt

HOW TO PREPARE

- Place the chives in a blender
- Add the oil
- Add the salt
- Blend until the chive is completely incorporated
- Strain the oil (optional)

### Tomato Oil

1 small can imported
  tomato paste
1 cup extra virgin olive oil

HOW TO PREPARE

- Combine the tomato paste and olive oil in a heavy-bottom saucepan
- Steep over low flame for 30 to 40 minutes, stirring occasionally—do not let it boil
- Skim off the oil and discard the paste

### Basil Oil

| | |
|---|---|
| 1 bunch basil (use small-leaf basil that has not yet flowered) | Small pinch of salt (helps to keep the basil green) |
| Slice garlic (optional) | 1 cup extra virgin olive oil (cold) |

HOW TO PREPARE

- Blanch the basil in boiling water for ½ minute and then shock in ice water
- Drain and wring out all of the water
- Chop the basil by hand
- Place in blender with garlic, salt, and cold olive oil
- Blend until the basil is completely incorporated
- Blend until smooth and strain

### Provençal Herb Oil

| | |
|---|---|
| ½ bunch thyme (preferably French) | ½ clove garlic |
| 1 sprig rosemary | 3 sprigs marjoram |
| | 1 cup extra virgin olive oil |

HOW TO PREPARE

- Warm the olive oil to about 170° and pour over the herbs
- Let steep for 2 to 3 days

Rub extra virgin olive oil on meats, poultry, and fish before cooking, and the natural juices will be sealed inside when roasting or grilling. Vegetables roasted with olive oil bring forth new tastes, textures, and delicate sweetness. Often combined with rosemary and a little garlic, roasting and basting with olive oil will add depth and richness to the final taste of meats and vegetables, and it's so easy to do.

---

### Roasting Vegetables with Olive Oil

Your favorite vegetables (for example: 2 new potatoes, 2 sweet potatoes, 1 onion, 2 carrots, 1 bell pepper)

Extra virgin olive oil
1 clove garlic, chopped
Sea salt
Pepper

HOW TO PREPARE

- Cut the vegetables into pieces and place in shallow baking dish
- Drizzle with extra virgin olive oil
- Add garlic, sea salt, and fresh pepper
- Roast for about an hour at 350°, stirring occasionally

NOTE: *You can use other vegetables (like zucchini, asparagus, or fennel); just make sure that whatever vegetables you use, you roast the root vegetables for about 30 minutes before adding the fast-cooking vegetables.*

## Cook with Olive Oil

### MAKE SAUCES WITH OLIVE OIL

Making sauces with olive oil adds to the taste, texture, and culinary enjoyment. In addition to the traditional uses for sauces, over pasta or for pizza, sauces can also be used over fish and meats or as dipping sauces for fried or roasted vegetables.

In addition to the family recipe (on page 56) for Tomato Sauce for Polenta (or Pasta or Ravioli), here are three more sauces from Erik, each using olive oil.

### Fresh Tomato Sauce with Black Olives

| | |
|---|---|
| 6 ripe tomatoes | ½ cup pitted oil-cured |
| Salt and pepper to taste | black olives |
| 2 cloves garlic, crushed | 6 anchovy fillets (optional) |
| ¾ cup extra virgin olive oil | |

#### HOW TO PREPARE

- Peel the tomatoes and cut in half
- Remove the seeds (with a spoon or your fingers) and season inside and out with salt, pepper, and garlic

- Grill the tomatoes over a hot grill with the cut side down for 3 minutes
- Remove from the grill and chop into very small pieces
- Dress with olive oil, olives, and anchovy (optional)

NOTE: *Use as a serving base for Grilled Marinated Calamari (see pages 196–197).*

## Romesco Sauce

| | |
|---|---|
| 10 toasted almonds | 1 cup extra virgin olive oil |
| 10 toasted hazelnuts | ½ cup bread crumbs |
| Pinch of chili flakes | Salt and pepper to taste |
| 1 clove garlic | |
| 3 each roasted red and yellow peppers | |

HOW TO PREPARE
- In a food processor, add nuts, chili flakes, and garlic clove and process
- Peel and seed the peppers
- Slowly add ½ cup of olive oil
- Add bread crumbs and then slowly add the rest of the olive oil
- Season with salt and pepper
- Serve with grilled fish or meats

NOTE: *A favorite at La Via Romana Restaurant in Bordighera, Liguria.*

### Salsa Verde

| | |
|---|---|
| ½ slice day-old bread | 2 bunches Italian flat parsley |
| 1 ounce red wine vinegar | 1½ cups extra virgin |
| 6 anchovy fillets | olive oil |
| ¼ cup capers | 4 hard-cooked eggs |
| 3 cloves garlic | Salt and pepper to taste |

HOW TO PREPARE

- Soak bread in water for 2 minutes and ring out excess moisture
- Place in food processor and dress with the vinegar
- Add anchovy fillets, capers, and garlic
- Process for 1 minute at high speed
- Add the parsley and process adding the olive oil slowly
- Remove from the food processor and place in a mixing bowl
- Separate the cooked egg whites and yolks, hand chopping each
- Then fold the separated whites and yolks into the mix and season with salt and pepper to taste

NOTE: *This sauce is served with grilled or steamed fish.*

---

### MARINATE WITH OLIVE OIL

There are several types of marinades, including acid-based (for example, lemon juice or wine), herb/spice-based, or oil-based. Marinades impart extra flavor to meats, chicken, and fish, and they do so because they not only lubricate the exterior of the food, but actually penetrate the food; this penetration process is made easier through the use of olive oil. Try the delicious recipe for Grilled Marinated Calamari with Fresh Tomato Sauce and Black Olives made famous by Erik and see how olive oil improves the overall flavor of this dish.

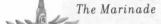

### The Marinade

| | |
|---|---|
| ½ bunch marjoram | 4 anchovy fillets |
| ½ bunch Italian flat parsley | Salt and pepper |
| 5 cloves garlic | ½ cup white wine |
| Chili flakes (just a pinch) | ½ cup extra virgin olive oil |
| 2 teaspoons cracked black pepper | |

HOW TO PREPARE

- In a food processor, add all the ingredients for the marinade, except the wine and the olive oil
- Process slowly, adding first the wine and then the olive oil

### Grilled Marinated Calamari with Fresh Tomato Sauce and Black Olives

| | |
|---|---|
| 4 pounds fresh calamari (cleaned) | Black Olives (see pages 193–194) |
| Fresh Tomato Sauce with | The Marinade (see above) |

- Skewer the calamari and cover with the marinade
- Marinate for 1 to 2 hours
- Remove from the marinade and season well with salt and pepper
- Char over a very hot grill
- Use the Fresh Tomato Sauce with Black Olives as a serving base for the calamari

---

The good news about marinades is that you can make a dish in advance and store it in oil for several days. This concept is similar to preserving food using olive oil.

### SAUTÉ/FRY WITH OLIVE OIL

It seems as if many recipes start with the following step: "Put ¼ cup olive oil in a skillet and place over medium heat." With the addition of a diced white onion and a clove of garlic, your kitchen will immediately be filled with a mouth-watering aroma. Olive oil is a suitable oil for frying (being four to five times more resistant to heat than seed oils or butter) and it can be heated to high temperatures without smoking. Another good point is that you need less oil in food preparation because olive oil actually increases in volume when heated. Also, heating olive oil does not affect its digestibility.

Therefore, it is perfect for frying since, unlike other vegetable oils, it actually coats the food rather than saturating it. This gives whatever food you are frying a crisp and caramelized crust—so delicious! Olive oil seals in the natural flavor of foods and can be filtered and reused as many as four times. This quality was very important to my relatives—things needed to be reused as much as possible. Since extra virgin olive oil has a lower smoke point, it's the best choice for dishes requiring sautéing.

At Rose Pistola restaurant in San Francisco, a favorite appetizer is Olive Oil Fried Zucchini Chips, the recipe for which Erik kindly provided. It uses green garlic—which is spring garlic—sweet, mild, with the appearance of a leek. If you can't find it, you can use your favorite garlic.

### Olive Oil–Fried Zucchini Chips with Green Garlic (SERVES 6)

2 large zucchini
Flour
Extra virgin olive oil (or
   blended 50/50 with
   canola oil)
2 tablespoons Italian flat
   parsley, 9 sprigs, chopped

2 tablespoons green garlic,
   shaved thin, or a
   chopped clove
Salt and pepper to taste

HOW TO PREPARE

- Slice the zucchini very thin on a mandolin (you should almost be able to see through them)
- Coat the zucchini with flour and shake off excess
- Put the oil in the fryer (about 3 inches)
- Slowly dunk the chips in the fryer in small batches
- Cook until very pale gold
- Put a paper towel on a plate
- Put the parsley and garlic on the paper towel

- Remove the chips and drain on the towel, where they will be coated with garlic and parsley
- Remove the paper
- Salt and pepper to taste

---

## BAKE WITH OLIVE OIL

While it may sound odd to some cooks, baking with olive oil has actually been done for centuries. Olive oil gives cakes and cookies a light texture and can be used with confidence in lieu of butter or other oils. Some cooks think that extra virgin olive oil has too dominant a flavor and will interfere with the taste of the end result. While the flavor of olive oil may add a desirable new dimension to your dessert or other baked goods, if you prefer not to have an olive taste, use a later harvest oil or, if you must, a light oil.

You can also use olive oil for preparing a baking pan/ dish before adding the dough or other mixture. Simply brush the oil onto your favorite baking dishes, pans, or cookie sheets.

Not surprisingly, my family often uses olive oil in their desserts. A favorite of mine is Castagnaccio, a sweet chestnut flour cake.

---

### Castagnaccio

| | |
|---|---|
| ½ cup raisins | ½ cup olive oil |
| 1 pound chestnut flour | 4 tablespoons pine nuts |
| A pinch of salt | 1 tablespoon fennel seeds |
| 4 cups carbonated water | (optional) |

- Preheat oven to 450°
- Soak the raisins in warm water for 20 minutes, drain, and damp dry
- Sift the flour into a large bowl, add a pinch of salt
- Add a small of amount of carbonated water and ¼ cup of the olive oil
- Mix slowly (preventing the formation of lumps)
- Add the rest of the carbonated water
- Add the pine nuts and the raisins
- Use the rest of the olive oil to coat a large, round baking dish (about 16 inches)
- Pour the mixture into the dish to a depth of about ½ inch
- Sprinkle with fennel seeds if using
- Bake for 15 to 20 minutes until firm but moist

Olive oil produces lighter-tasting baked goods and allows the flavor of the other ingredients to come forth. Because olive oil contains vitamin E, it helps to maintain the freshness of baked goods and creates moist cakes, biscuits, and muffins. It can even be used in making ice cream. A unique way to top off a delicious meal, according to Erik, is to serve an olive oil cake and olive oil ice cream!

## Olive Oil Cake

| | |
|---|---|
| 3½ cups flour | 6 tablespoons milk |
| 3 tablespoons baking powder | 2 tablespoons lemon juice |
| 2 cups sugar | 7 ounces melted butter |
| Zest from 3 lemons | 1⅓ cups extra virgin olive oil |
| 6 eggs | Powdered sugar (optional) |

### HOW TO PREPARE

- Preheat oven to 350° and lightly oil a 9-inch cake pan or loaf pan
- Using a mixer, combine dry ingredients and blend slowly
- Add lemon zest, eggs, milk, and lemon juice at medium-low speed
- Combine melted butter and olive oil, then slowly add to batter until thoroughly blended
- Pour into baking pan and bake for 55 to 60 minutes (until it's dark brown and passes the clean-skewer test)
- You may wish to dust the top with powered sugar for presentation

## Olive Oil Ice Cream

| | |
|---|---|
| 10 egg yolks | 2 cups milk |
| 1¼ cups granulated sugar | 2 cups cream |
| 3½ ounces olive oil | |

- Beat the egg yolks and gradually add the sugar
- Add the olive oil, milk, and cream and mix
- Put in an ice cream maker and follow prefreezing and mixing directions
- If you do not have an ice cream machine, put the mixture in the freezer, take it out and mix every 20 minutes until it acquires the creamy texture of ice cream

---

## USE OLIVE OIL INSTEAD OF BUTTER

To help you in determining how to substitute olive oil in baking or other cooking recipes, here is a handy conversion chart to substitute olive oil for batter in recipes:

| Butter/Margarine | Olive Oil |
|---|---|
| 1 teaspoon | 3/4 teaspoon |
| 1 tablespoon | 2¼ teaspoons |
| ¼ cup | 3 tablespoons |
| ⅓ cup | ¼ cup |
| ½ cup | ¼ cup + 2 tablespoons |
| ⅔ cup | ½ cup |
| ¾ cup | ½ cup + 1 tablespoon |
| 1 cup | 3/4 cup |

*Preserve with It, Mist It,*
*Freeze It, Store It*

### PRESERVE FOOD IN OLIVE OIL

For centuries, particularly before the arrival of refrigeration, people used olive oil to preserve meats, fish, vegetables, cheeses, and even to seal wine. Olive oil provides a seal that can delay oxidation, deterioration, and mold.

Erik's fish recipe for Olive Oil–Preserved Fish can be made in advance and stored in oil for up to five days. He advises always to use food-safe or nonreactive containers (either stainless steel, ceramic, or glass) and not aluminum or iron when preparing or storing any food that contains acid. Erik also notes that the cured fish would not be very good if cooked and to "think of it as a cerviche that is 'cooked' by the acid in the wine and lemon juice."

---

*Olive Oil–Preserved Fish*   (SERVES 6)

| | |
|---|---|
| 3 pounds salmon fillet | 4 bay leaves |
| 1½ cups dry white wine | Extra virgin olive oil to cover |
| 1½ cups white wine vinegar | Capers |
|    or fresh lemon juice | Fresh herbs (basil, dill, or |
| 2 tablespoons salt |    tarragon) |

HOW TO PREPARE

- Slice the salmon about ⅛ inch thick
- Mix together the wine, vinegar, salt, and bay leaves

- Add the salmon, one slice at a time, to the marinade
- Let cure in the marinade for 2 hours
- Drain and pat dry with a paper towel
- Arrange the slices on a serving platter and cover with olive oil
- Sprinkle with capers and fresh herbs and serve (or save)
- Serve with focaccia and a dish of olives

NOTE: *This recipe can be used for all types of fresh fish, including fresh sardines, anchovies, and halibut (to name a few)*

---

A "preserved" fish (that is cooked) and that we are all familiar with is canned tuna fish, whether it is in oil or salt and water. However, an excellent way to prepare tuna, which can be stored and used for salads and sandwiches (or panini), is offered by Erik in his recipe for Tuna Confit.

---

### Tuna Confit

| | |
|---|---|
| 3 pounds fresh albacore or tombo tuna loin | 3 tablespoons salt |
| 5 sprigs marjoram | 4–5 crushed garlic cloves |
| 1 sprig rosemary | 1 whole lemon, sliced |
| 2 teaspoons cracked black pepper | 1 cup dry white wine |
| | Extra virgin olive oil to cover |

HOW TO PREPARE

- Cut the tuna into three 1-pound pieces
- Take the herbs, pepper, salt, crushed garlic, and lemon and

place on a heavy cutting board and chop together just enough to bruise the herbs and evenly distribute the salt and cracked pepper

- Rub the tuna with the mixture and place in a nonreactive dish or pan
- Cover with the remaining herb-salt mix
- Let sit for 2 hours
- Add the wine and cover with olive oil
- The tuna can be cooked in two ways or you can use a combination of both: On the stovetop over a low flame for 20 minutes or in a 350° oven for 1 hour
- After cooking let cool
- Store in an airtight food-safe container covered with the remaining olive oil from the selected cooking process
- This is *far* better than any canned tuna!

The following recipe, once again from Erik, combines both the Tuna Confit and the Salsa Verde (see page 195).

## Ligurian Inspired Tuna Salad (SERVES 6)

½ cup fresh fava beans, peeled

½ cup fresh baby peas

6 small shaved artichokes

1 bunch arugula

1 bulb shaved fennel

10 + basil leaves

10 + Italian flat parsley leaves

3 tablespoons brined capers

10 oil-packed anchovies cut into small pieces

24 + small black olives in brine (Taggia, Gaeta, or Niçoise)

24 ounces Tuna Confit

Red wine vinegar

Salt and pepper to taste

6 tablespoons Salsa Verde

Six 10-minute hard-cooked eggs, peeled and cut in half

### HOW TO PREPARE

- In a mixing bowl, combine the fava beans, vegetables, and herbs
- Add the capers, anchovies, and olives
- Toss well with the herb oil from the Tuna Confit
- Lightly dress with red wine vinegar and season well with salt and pepper
- Serve in a large bowl or on individual plates
- Top with the Tuna Confit crumbles
- Top with Salsa Verde and egg halves

NOTE: *You may vary the recipe according to which vegetables are in season.*

Fill a plastic spray bottle with your favorite extra virgin olive oil and spray it into a pan, saucepan, or griddle for great sautéing and stir-frying results. An olive oil spray bottle sprays the oil in a focused stream; for a different spray pattern, you can try a mist sprayer. I prefer the spray bottle and mist sprayer to commercially prepared cooking sprays, which contain propellants and chemical additives. One of my favorite uses of the sprayer is to prepare a pan for scrambling eggs in the morning. Wait until you taste the difference!

### FREEZE OLIVE OIL FOR A BUTTERLIKE SUBSTITUTE

Olive oil can be used in place of butter as a spread. Use the plastic top of a butter dish or part of an ice cube tray to freeze olive oil, or pour the oil into a plastic bowl or very small rectangular pan and freeze. When the oil solidifies, store it in the refrigerator. Use the firm olive oil as a spread instead of butter when serving bread, baked potatoes, other vegetables, and anything else on which you usually spread butter—your heart will thank you.

### STORE OLIVE OIL—REMEMBER "OLIO NUOVO, VINO VECCHIO"

There is an old Italian proverb—"*olio nuovo, vino vecchio*" (it is best to consume "young oil" but "old wine"). Properly stored, olive oil will keep longer than other edible oils—up to two years. However, once opened, olive oil should optimally be used within sixty to ninety days. The best containers for olive oil are dark glass, stainless steel, or tin. Make sure the container can be resealed tightly. Store olive oil in a cool, dark place away from light and heat.

There will be a "use by" date on the olive oil you purchase, though with all of the different uses described in this book, I can't imagine anyone having a problem with the bottle of olive oil exceeding its recommended shelf life! A more likely scenario is that you will run out of it on a fairly regular basis!

# CHAPTER TWELVE

# Let's Hear from You!

NOW THAT I HAVE shared with you over a hundred ways you can use olive oil in your daily life, I would like to know if *you* have any tips or secret recipes that you would like to share. I know that around the world, there are a great many olive oil aficionados—many people who are as passionate as I am. After reading this book, I hope you count yourself among this ever-increasing number. As you try my suggested uses, do let me know if you have your own favorite uses for olive oil, special family recipes or formulas, or, if you have a particular favorite olive oil, let me know its name. I welcome the opportunity to hear from you! Simply e-mail me at olives@thepassionateolive.com.

In this last chapter, I would like to offer just a few more tips and suggestions. The first deals with the inevitability of some olive oil stains, the second covers a safety issue, and the third is the note of caution that I mentioned in the health chapter.

First, just what does one do about olive oil stains? Okay, oil is oil, and it can stain fabric. Here are some "tricks" that I've learned (for washable fabrics) to take care of any oil or grease stain on clothes or bed and table linens. A tip from my mother is to gently rub baking soda into the spot, let it sit overnight, then brush the baking soda off and wash normally. The baking soda will absorb the oil out of the fabric. Another tip—this one from Angela—to remove olive oil stains (again for washable fabrics) is to rub the spot with Savon de Marseille or a block of white laundry soap, and then wash. And still another is to spray the soiled area with Fantastik and wash. For fabrics that require dry cleaning, my dry cleaner assures me that oil is easily removed from fabrics during the dry-cleaning process. If you have a "secret" formula that rids clothing and/or linens of oily spots, I would be very interested in hearing about it.

Second, remember safety. I want to be certain, now that you are ready to use olive oil in so many different ways, that you use it safely, particularly when bathing. Remember, oil is oil and is by nature slippery. When using it in a relaxing or romantic bath, be careful—particularly when you enter or exit the tub. A slip or fall would surely cancel all those feelings of relaxation or romance that you originally set out to attain. So, please watch your step!

And, third, a note of caution. Many of the ideas and tips included in *The Passionate Olive: 101 Things to Do with Olive Oil* have been handed down in my family for generations. While I've done a great deal of research to verify the accuracy of the content, my intent is not to prescribe cures. The information provided in my book is *not* intended in any way to be a substitute for professional medical or health advice, diagnosis, or treatment. Do not use the information here to diagnose or treat a health problem or illness without consulting your pediatrician, gynecologist, dermatologist, internist, family doctor, veterinarian, or any of your other doctors. There is no substitute for sound medical advice.

That said, enjoy your adventure with olive oil and let me hear from you! And whenever you have the opportunity to ask any wise Italian, Greek, Spanish, or other Mediterranean native about olive oil, mention this book and some of the uses. *They will probably have 101 more!*

# Olive Oil
# Usage Guidelines

I AM OFTEN ASKED about my favorite olive oils, and each time I hesitate because . . . first of all I must ask: "For what use?" Is it for drizzling on food or cooking? For around the house? For massaging your partner or the dog? I generally use extra virgin olive oil for most everything; however, check the following charts, Suggested Types of Olive Oil for 100 Uses and Suggested Types of Olive Oil for Cooking, and, using your own judgment, you will discover what is best for you.

The next question is: What is your favorite extra virgin olive oil? I answer that one's preference in olive oil is really a matter of personal taste. I know people who buy *only* one specific brand of extra virgin olive oil; I am more experimental in my approach. I belong to several olive oil clubs and receive different imported estate olive oils and olive oils from California each month. I also buy olive oil from producers and retailers that I know and trust. My favorite tends to be a high-intensity extra virgin olive oil, in terms of fruitiness, bitterness, and pungency.

*Some Guidelines for Buying Extra Virgin Olive Oil*

1. Always check for a producing country's seal of authenticity—for example, the COOC from California; DOP from Italy; AOC from France; DOP from Greece; DO from Spain.
2. Check the "use by" date.
3. Check for the winners of olive oil competitions—for example, the worldwide competition, hosted each year at the Los Angeles County Fair. These oils will have additional seals, signifying Gold, Silver, and Bronze medals on the bottles.

*My Best Advice*

Ask the official tasters at olive oil competitions (by checking the award results online), or quiz your trusted retailer. Then, after experimenting and tasting, ask yourself . . . what do you personally like?

# SUGGESTED TYPES OF OLIVE OIL FOR 100 USES

| | OLIVE OIL | | |
|---|---|---|---|
| **CHAPTERS AND USES** | **EXTRA VIRGIN OLIVE OIL\*** | **VIRGIN OLIVE OIL** | **OLIVE OIL** |
| AROUND THE HOUSE | 4, 5 | 10, 12, 13 | 1, 2, 3, 6, 7, 8, 9, 10, 11, 12, 13, 14, 15, 16, 17, 18, 19, 20, 21, 22, 23, 24, 25, 26 |
| TO YOUR HEALTH | 27, 28, 29, 30, 31, 32, 33, 34, 35, 37, 40, 43, 44 | 36, 37, 41, 42, 43, 44 | 36, 38, 39, 41, 42, 43, 44, 45 |
| BEAUTY IS SKIN DEEP | 46, 47, 48, 49, 50, 51, 52, 53, 54, 55, 56, 57, 60, 62, 63, 64 | 50, 51, 52, 56, 58, 59, 61 | 52, 58, 59, 61 |
| OLIVE OIL AND SENSUALITY | 65, 66, 67 | | |
| PREGNANCY AND BABY CARE | 68, 69, 70, 71, 72, 73, 74 | | |
| CARE AND FEEDING OF PETS | 75, 76, 77, 78, 81, 82 | 78, 83 | 78, 79, 80, 83, 84 |
| RITUAL AND RELIGION | 85, 86, 87, 88, 89, 90, 91 | | |
| PARTIES AND SPECIAL OCCASIONS | 92, 93, 94, 96, 97, 98, 99, 100 | 98, 99 | 95, 98, 99 |

*\* I tend to use extra virgin olive oil for everything!*

## SUGGESTED TYPES OF OLIVE OIL FOR COOKING

| | OLIVE OIL | | |
|---|---|---|---|
| **COOKING USES** | **EXTRA VIRGIN OLIVE OIL*** | **VIRGIN OLIVE OIL** | **OLIVE OIL** |
| BAKING | X<br>low intensity | X | X |
| FRYING/SAUTÉING (Olive oil's smoke point is around 410° F, with a high-end extra virgin olive oil at around 375° F) | X<br>best for sautéing | X<br>good for sautéing | X<br>often recommended for stir-frying and deep frying |
| DRIZZLING DIRECTLY ON FOOD AS A CONDIMENT | X<br>high intensity | | |
| FISH AND POULTRY | X<br>medium to high intensity | | |
| MARINADES | X<br>medium to high intensity | | |
| MEATS | X<br>high intensity | | |
| PASTA | X<br>medium to high intensity | | |
| ROASTING | X<br>medium to high intensity | | |
| SAUCES NOTE: MAYONNAISE** | X<br>low to medium intensity | | |
| SALADS | X<br>medium to high intensity | | |

* As I've mentioned, I tend to use extra virgin olive oil for everything! I like a high-intensity olive oil—fruity, bitter, and pungent, excerpt for baking.
**For making mayonnaise, it is best to use a late-harvest or low-intensity yellow olive oil.

# Olive Oil
## Retail Resources

SPECIALTY STORES FOR OLIVE OIL
AND OLIVE OIL PRODUCTS

*The following list includes a selection of specialty stores that I have visited in the United States for olive oil and products. Please let me know of the names and addresses of specialty stores where you find olive oil and olive oil products. You can e-mail me at olives@thepassionateolive.com.*

**Corti Brothers**
5180 Folsom Boulevard
Sacramento, CA 95819
Tel: 916-736-3800
Fax: 916-736-3807
www.cortibros.biz

**Katz and Company**
101 South Coombs, Y-3
Napa, CA 94559
Tel: 800-676-7176
Fax: 707-254-1846
www.katzandco.com

**Dean & DeLuca**
Check website for store
locations
Tel: 800-221-7714
Fax: 800-781-4050
www.dean-deluca.com

**L'Occitane**
Check website for store
locations
Tel: 888-623-2880
www.loccitane.com

*Oliviers & Co.*
Check website for store
locations
Tel: 877-828-6620
www.oliviersandco.com

*Sur La Table*
Check website for store
locations
Tel: 800-243-0852
www.surlatable.com

*The Olive Press*
14301 Arnold Drive
Glen Ellen, CA 95442
Tel: 800-965-4839
Fax: 707-939-8999
www.theolivepress.com

*The Pasta Shop*
5655 College Avenue
Oakland, CA 94618
Tel: 510-652-0462
Fax: 510-601-8251
www.markethallfoods.com

*Trader Joe's*
Check website for store
locations
Tel: 800-746-7857
www.traderjoes.com

*We Olive*
1311 Park Street
Paso Robles, CA 93446
Tel: 805-239-7667
www.weolive.com

*Whole Foods Market*
Check website for store
locations
Tel: 512-477-4455
www.wholefoodsmarket.com

*Williams-Sonoma*
Check website for store
locations
Tel: 800-541-2233
www.williams-sonoma.com

*Zabar's*
2245 Broadway (at 80th Street)
New York, NY 10024
Tel: 212-787-2000
Fax: 212-580-4477
www.zabars.com

*The following list includes a selection of the olive oil mills and producers in California. For a complete list visit www.cooc.com.*

*Apollo Olive Oil*
P.O. Box 1054
Oregon House, CA 95962
Tel: 530-692-2314
Fax: 530-692-0840
www.apollooliveoil.com

*B. R. Cohn Olive Oil Co.*
15000 Sonoma Highway
Glen Ellen, CA 95442
Tel: 707-933-9675
Fax: 707-938-4585
www.brcohn.com

*California Olive Ranch*
2675 Lone Tree Road
Oroville, CA 95965
Tel: 530-846-8000
Fax: 530-846-8003
www.californiaoliveranch.com

*Calolea Olive Oil*
11343 Choctaw Trail
Loma Rica, CA 95901
Tel: 530-749-1240
www.calolea.com

*Figueroa Farms*
1801 Fletcher Way
Santa Ynez, CA 93460
Tel: 805-686-4890
Fax: 805-686-2887
www.figueroafarms.com

*Frantoio Ristorante &*
*Olive Oil Co.*
152 Shoreline Highway
Mill Valley, CA 94941
Tel: 415-289-5777
Fax: 415-289-5775
www.frantoio.com

*Le Colline di Santa Cruz*
1535 Valencia Road
Aptos, CA 95003
Tel: 831-662-2345
Fax: 831-475-9157
www.santacruzolive.com

*McEvoy Ranch*
5935 Red Hill Road
Petaluma, CA 94952
Tel: 707-778-2307
Fax: 707-778-0128
www.mcevoyranch.com

*Olivas de Oro Olive Company*
P.O. Box 320518
Los Gatos, CA 95032
Tel: 408-353-1229
Fax: 408-353-1529
www.olivasdeoro.com

*Olivinia, LLC*
4555 Arroyo Road
Livermore, CA
Tel: 925-455-8710
Fax: 925-447-2945
www.theolivina.com

*Round Pond*
877 Rutherford Crossroad
Rutherford, CA 94573
Tel: 877-963-9364
Fax: 707-763-7544
www.roundpond.com

*Stella Cadente Olive Oil Company*
P.O. Box 160
Boonville, CA 95415
Tel: 707-895-2848
Fax: 707-895-9556
www.stellacadente.com

*Stonehouse California Olive Oil*
675 Cedar Street
Berkeley, CA 94710
Tel: 800-865-4836
www.stonehouseoliveoil.com

*Willow Creek Olive Ranch*
8530 Vineyard Drive
Paso Robles, CA 93446
Tel: 805-227-0186
Fax: 805-237-9181
www.willowcreekoliveranch.com

## OLIVE OIL FROM ITALY, SPAIN, GREECE, AND FRANCE*

*The following list includes some olive oil brands that I know and like from different regions in Italy, Spain, Greece, and France. Please let me know of the names of olive oils that you like. You can e-mail me at olives@thepassionateolive.com.*

## Italy

### Abruzzo
Olio di San Martino

### Calabria
L'Aspromontano

### Lazio
Merlano
Silvi Sabina Sapori

### Liguria
Ardoino
Isnardi
Roi
Le Due Baie

### Marché
Petrini

### Molise
Colavita
Louianna

### Puglia
Masseries di Santeramo

*For other brands and for olive oil from Turkey, Australia, New Zealand, and other olive oil–producing countries, check the specialty stores listed on pages 223–224 or the selected websites (pages 233–234).

*Sardinia*
Ottidoro

*Sicily*
Ravida
Fontanasalsa

*Tuscany*
Badia a Coltibuono
Badia al Guardo
Laudemio (various producers)
VR Extra Virgin Olive Oil
Volpaia

*Umbria*
Mancianti
Monini
Sinoleum

*Catalonia*
Antara
Gasull
L'Estornell
Pons
Unio

*Castilla-La Mancha*
Zoe

# Greece

*Peloponnesus*
Lykovouno

*Crete*
Psillakis Biojoy
Sitia

# Spain

*Andalusia*
Caroliva
Columela
Molino De Leoncio Gomez
Nuñez de Prado
Solero Romero

# France

Alziari Olive Oil
Chateau Virant
Moulin Saint Michel
Oliviers & Co. (various producers)

*Annotated Selected Websites*

### Awards/Education/Events

http://lacountyfair.com
> *Check the annual Olive Oil of the World awards; since the competition is associated with the Wine of the World awards, add to the web address a forward slash (/), the word (wine), and the annual date you wish to check, e.g., 2006.*

www.extension.ucdavis.edu
> *For the Sensory Evaluation of Olive Oil course where you will learn how to evaluate olive oils by tasting recently released olive oils from California and Europe.*

www.copia.org
> *COPIA, located in Napa, California, brings enthusiasts together with leading vintners, chefs, gardeners and artists to explore and celebrate wine, food, gardens and the arts.*

www.olivefestival.com
> *An annual festival (December–February) is held in Sonoma, California. The festival highlights the beautiful Season of the Olive, from harvest to press.*

www.oliveoil.org

> *Located in Imperia, Italy, the ONAOO (Organizzazione Nazionale Assaggiatori Olio di Oliva—the National Organization for the Tasting of Olive Oil) was formed in 1983. As the first official organization to offer courses to certify olive oil–tasting panel judges throughout the world, the ONAOO is highly recognized. Course information, documents, and news items are provided on the website.*

www.oliveoilsource.com

> *A complete and comprehensive source of anything related to olive oil—what it is, who makes it, who's who, tours, and olive-picking opportunities. It is here that you can also find out about worldwide events and even how to make olive oil soap.*

## Health

www.care2.com

> *An environmental network for "healthy people and a healthy planet."*

www.headliceinfo.com

> *Highlights the olive oil cure for head lice!*

www.health911.com

> *An informative alternative medicine site with hundreds of remedies, protocols, and information to help you maintain good health.*

## Olive Oil Museums . . . that I have visited in Italy

www.lungarotti.com

> *Housed in a restored medieval dwelling and situated in the historic center of Torgiano, Umbria, the Lungarotti Museo*

dell'Olivo e dell'Olio *(Olive and Olive Oil Museum)* consists of eleven rooms providing a wealth of information ranging from specific cultivars to traditional presses and water-powered mills to the fascinating uses of olive oil in everyday life.

www.museodellolivo.com

*Housed in a beautiful Art Nouveau building, constructed during the 1920s for the Fratelli Carli Corporation, the Museo dell'Olivo (Olive Tree Museum) was awarded the European Museum of the Year award in 1993, the year it opened. The museum portrays the olive tree as a symbol of the Mediterranean and highlights the leading role it has played in the economic, technical, artistic, and religious history of humanity.*

www.museum.it

*Located in Cisano di Bardolino on Lake Garda, the Museo Dell'Olio D'Oliva (Olive Oil Museum) exhibits a collection of antique items that were used in olive mills from the 1700s to the beginning of the twentieth century. As the first initiative of its kind, the museum, which opened in 1987, has examples of antique lever presses and more recent machinery.*

www.oliosommariva.it

*A delightful and friendly small museum (Antico Frantoio Sommariva) is situated in the old medieval walls of the city of Albenga. Within its stone vaulted-roof rooms are collections of amphoras, tools, machines, and objects used in the past to improve the cultivation of the olive tree and the production of olive oil.*

www.sabina.it

*Located in the medieval city of Castlenuovo di Farfa, the Museo Dell'Olio della Sabina (Olive Oil Museum of Sabina) is a unique museum that is a fascinating sensory experience. Five world-renowned artists celebrate and interpret the significance and traditions of olive oil and its presence in contemporary society though sculpture, art, and music.*

www.sistemamuseo.it
*Located within the medieval city of Trevi, known as the Olive Oil Capital of Italy, the Museo della Civiltá dell'Ulivo (Museum of the Civilization of the Olive Tree) is an educational adventure with videos, artifacts, wall panels with explanations, cartoons, and interactive quizzes.*

## Olive Oil Lamps

www.lehmans.com
*For an olive oil chamber lamp.*

www.phoenixrising-pt.com
*For an Elazar olive oil lamp.*

## Organizations

www.cooc.com
*A wealth of information (frequently asked questions, current news, and events) from the COOC (California Olive Oil Council) is located here. Founded in 1992, the mission of the COOC is to make California a source of world-class olive oil and to exchange information about growing olives and making olive oil. Its membership is open to all interested consumers, as well as olive oil producers.*

www.internationaloliveoil.org
*Learn about the IOOC's (International Olive Oil Council) charter, classifications of olive oil, and important international guidelines related to olive oil. Created in 1956 and located in Madrid, Spain, the IOOC is an intergovernmental organization in charge of administering the International Olive Oil Agreement.*

*Restaurants*

www.kokkari.com

> *Kokkari is located in San Francisco, California. It features elegant, rustic and exquisite Greek cuisine. An inviting fireplace, extensive woodwork, hand-made pottery and freshly picked flowers all reflect the warmth and tradition of old-world charm. Erik Cosselmon, who contributed recipes to this book, is the executive chef.*

www.frantoio.com

> *Frantoio Ristorante and Olive Oil Co. in Mill Valley, California, is the only restaurant in the United States with an in-house state-of-the-art olive-oil-production facility.*

www.kuletos.com

> *A local favorite right off Union Square, Kuleto's is a combination of old San Francisco aura, Italian conviviality, and contemporary vitality.*

*Additional Information and Products*

www.italiancookingandliving.com

> *Italian Cooking and Living and the Italian Culinary Center in New York, through the Italian Olive Oil and Specialty Food Center, hosts an olive oil club, offers a course in olive oil, and suggests fine Italian olive oils.*

www.oliveoilfromspain.com

> *Spain is the leading olive oil–producing country. This site focuses on the large variety of flavors, aromas, colors, and textures of Spanish olive oils.*

www.huiles-de-provence.com

> *Detailed information about olive oil producers from France.*

Educationally rich and comprehensive, this site highlights the characteristics, taste, and authenticity of selected olive oils.

www.egebirlik.org.tr

Learn about olives and olive oils from Turkey. The website includes interesting information on Turkish olive oil production, the varieties of Turkish olives, exporters, and Turkish cuisine.

www.oliveoil.gr

Greece is the world's largest consumer per capita of olive oil and the third-largest olive oil–producing country. This informative site is the home of SEVITEL, the Greek Association of Industries and Processors of Olive Oil. It includes a list of several olive oil producers and exporters and promotes Greek olive oil in the international market in cooperation with the Hellenic Foreign Trade Board (HEPO).

www.australianolives.com/au

The Australian Olive Association promotes the development of the national olive industry in Australia. The website is a good place to find out about Australian olive oil.

www.DHCcare.com

DHC's complete skin care collection is based on virgin olive oil and other beneficial botanicals. Discover age-defying treatments that blend the best of nature with the latest innovations in science.

www.olivesnz.org.nz

The New Zealand Olive Association, now Olives New Zealand was fomed in 1992 to promote olive growing and production, to provide a platform for an interchange of ideas and to undertake research and to set industry standards.

# Selected Bibliography

Barilla, Jean. *Olive Oil Miracle*. New Canaan, Conn.: Keats Publishing, 1996.

Barranco, Diego. *El Cultivo del Olivo*. Madrid: Ediciones Mundi-Prensa, 1998.

Baussan, Olivier, and Jacques Chibois. *Olive Oil, A Gourmet Guide*. Paris: Flammarion, 2000.

Bickers, Merry. *I Didn't Know That Olive Oil Would Burn!* Wolf Creek, Ore.: Merry Corliss, 1999.

Carli, Carlo, et al. *Museo dell'Olivo*. Bergamo: Poligrafische Bolis S.p.A, 1994.

Chiarello, Michael. *Flavored Oils*. San Francisco: Chronicle Books, 1995.

Cunningham, Scott. *Cunningham's Encyclopedia of Magical Herbs*. St. Paul: Llewellyn Publications, 1998.

———. *Magical Aromatherapy*. St. Paul: Llewellyn Publications, 1994.

Debarry, Nicolas. *The Little Book of Olive Oil*. Paris: Flammarion, 1999.

Dolamore, Anne. *The Essential Olive Oil Companion*. London: Grub Street, 1994.

Downie, David. *Enchanted Liguria*. New York: Rizzoli International Publications, 1997.

Dudley, Martin, and Geoffrey Rowell. *The Oil of Gladness.* London: Liturgical Press. 1993.

Kiritsakis, Apostolos. *Olive Oil: From the Tree to the Table.* 2nd Edition. Trumbull, Conn.: Food and Nutrition Press, 1998.

Klein, Margaret Blyth. *The Feast of the Olive.* San Francisco: Chronicle Books, 1994.

Knickerbocker, Peggy. *Olive Oil: From Tree to Table.* San Francisco: Chronicle Books, 1997.

Lungarotti, Maria Grazia Marchetti. *Olive and Oil Museum Itinerary.* Torgiano: Fondazione Lungarotti, 2000.

Midgley, John. *The Goodness of Olive Oil.* London: Pavilion Books Limited, 1992.

Moritz, Andreas. *The Amazing Liver Cleanse.* Bloomington, Ind: AuthorHouse, 2002.

Pickford, Louise. *The Olive Oil Cookbook.* New York: Smithmark Publishers, 1994.

Plotkin, Fred. *Recipes from Paradise.* New York: Little, Brown and Company, 1997.

Quatrochi, Kathlyn. *The Skin Care Book: Simple Herbal Recipes.* New York: Interweave Press, 1997.

Rogers, Ford. *Olives: Cooking with Olives and Their Oils.* Berkeley: Ten Speed Press, 1995.

Shaw, Jerry. *The Healing Power of Olive Oil.* Boca Raton, Fla.: Globe Communications Corp., 1997.

Stewart, Kimberly L. "Virtuosity: Extra Virgin Olive Oil Is Divine," *Better Nutrition,* February 2003, pages 46–51.

Taylor, Judith. *The Olive in California.* Berkeley: Ten Speed Press, 2000.

Tindall, Bruce, and Mark Watson. *How Does Olive Oil Lose Its Virginity?* New York: William Morrow, 1994.

Weinzweig, Ari. *A Guide to Good Olive Oil.* Ann Arbor, Mich.: Zingerman's, 1995.

# Index

*Chef: Erik Cosselmon*

Erik Cosselmon is the executive chef of Kokkari Estiatorio in San Francisco, California. Cosselmon graduated with honors from the Culinary Institute of America in Hyde Park, New York, and worked in the south of France, in New York at restaurants such as Tavern on the Green, 44 at the Royalton Hotel, Le Bernardin, and Daniel, and in San Francisco at Rose Pistola, where as executive chef he helped make it one of the most celebrated dining destinations in California. A creative and dedicated chef, Cosselmon's elegantly rustic and full-flavored cuisine showcases seasonal ingredients.

*Illustrator: Margie L. Preston*

Margie L. Preston, dba Interlace Design at www.interlacedesign.com, is a talented and experienced artist and web and print designer. Margie captures her clients' passion for every project. She combines her love of art with her knowledge and experience in electronic graphics to produce professional, creative, and engaging results.